Drinking From The Nile

Drinking From The Nile

Twelve Years In Sudan

a memoir

Sheila Van der Smissen

Images © Sheila Van der Smissen
Map design by Linda Zupcic, Blue Oak Art
Cover design by Pamela Foster Mullins, P.M. Design

Back Cover: Zehir—a conical red clay pot containing drinking water from the Nile River. Evaporation through the clay cools the water. Frequently found on the streets of Khartoum, zehirs are placed under shady trees. A plastic cup for dipping and drinking is available for all to use.

ISBN-978-1-6720381-1-9

To Isabelle

My story, our stories
As I remember

*"You have brains in your head. You have feet in your
shoes. You can steer yourself any direction you choose.
You're on your own. And you know what you know. And
YOU are the one who'll decide where to go..."*
—Dr. Seuss, *"Oh, The Places You'll Go!"*

Once you drink from the Nile, you will come back again.
—A Sudanese Proverb

Table of Contents

Part One

Part Two

Prologue

I heard giggles from the cloakroom; the boys were looking at bare breasts again. It was recess time in the fifth grade. If my teacher, Mr. Riley, found the boys, would he remove that *National Geographic* from the bookshelf? I hope he doesn't hear their chuckles because I liked to look at those magazines—and the nearly naked men. I also gazed in wonderment at the pictures of exotic places. My curiosity was aroused. How can people and places be so different, different than our family, our community? How they live, how they look, how they dress (or don't), wear their hair, and paint their faces. I wonder if Mr. Riley even knows the magazines contain nudity.

National Geographic—so much more than the near-naked bodies of brown people. My young heart soared. Wanderlust was born. I wanted to go to those places.

I was born in the 1940s. Was I too late? Had I missed my real generation? I should have been born in the time of Captain Cook and Dr. Livingstone... and been a man. Will there be anything left to discover when I grow up?

The tropical countries spoke to me. I wondered what it would be like to swing through the jungle on vines. I wanted to live in a hut surrounded by trees reaching for the sky—trees so tall I'd fall over backward just looking up. I wanted to swim in the warm turquoise waters and spear a fish for dinner. I wanted to sit on a beach the color of sugar and dry off in the cool breeze under the gently swaying palm trees. And I wanted to shimmy up one of those trees and pick a coconut.

I wanted to trudge across the dunes of the African desert to sell my camels. I wanted to watch the king of the beasts chase a gazelle. I dreamed of ascending the snowy mountain peaks of the Himalayas with my yaks and Sherpa friends. I hoped to stroll through the ancient bazaars in the Middle East and find treasures in corners of dusty shops. I'd climb to the top of an Egyptian pyramid. I'd dive in the Great Barrier Reef. I'd brew tea over an open wood fire in China. Could I be the next Margaret Mead? Live with natives, study different cultures, document social customs? Curiosity filled me; who we are and how we, the human family, can be so diverse.

CRISO

One Christmas, when we were in grammar school, my sister Charlotte and I were given a globe for our shared bedroom. I would sit in front of it, close my eyes, spin the globe, and drag my finger on it until it stopped. Eyes open, I'd say the name of the country and dream of going there.

I grew up in a small farming community near Fresno in the San Joaquin Valley, the middle of California. I thought we were poor. In third grade, I was the last child to have a television set at home. By that time, I had missed half of the *I Love Lucy* series. My parents drove the oldest car in the neighborhood. Looking back, I realize we were firmly middle class. But as a child, I wondered what opportunity I would have to travel the world. Vacations for my family meant camping nearby in the Sierra Nevada Mountains.

Could I escape? See the world? Doubtful. And yet, I held fast to my dreams.

CRISO

In 1956 when I was ten years old, a class assignment was what we wanted to be when we grew up. I wanted to be a chemist and work in a pharmacy. However, during my research, a pharmacist told me that it was not a profession for women. A pharmacy was a business; one needed commercial skills in addition to knowledge of chemistry. Women didn't do that in the 1950s. He suggested I become a laboratory technologist; therefore, I wrote about working in a clinical laboratory. The profession sounded interesting, included chemistry, and I decided to follow that career path. At that early age, I made a plan and stuck to it. I needed a college degree. I would be the first in my extended family to attend college. I wish I could go back now and show that pharmacist my M.B.A.

CRSO

In 1968, a Bachelor of Science degree in hand, I applied for medical technology internships in Southern California. I could have done the program at a hospital in Fresno, my home town, yet I purposely chose not to apply there. I wanted to get out—away from home, away from the farming community, away from the familiar. I was accepted for the one year program at the University of California, Irvine Medical Center. I packed up my car, destination Disneyland. A small apartment in Orange County would be my home, a few miles from the happiest place on earth.

As in nursing, laboratory personnel were mostly women; young, carefree, and well paid. My ears perked up when I heard my colleagues talk about their travels to Hawaii, the Caribbean, and especially to Europe. When I saw their photos of the Eiffel Tower, the Coliseum, and Buckingham Palace, I pictured myself there.

Could I do the same? Travel to Europe? See the sights I had dreamed about? Touch the Leaning Tower of Pisa, stroll the Champs-Élysées, hear the chimes of Big Ben? Visit the places I had seen in magazines?

I completed my year of training, passed my state and national exams the week the Apollo Mission landed on the moon; and therefore, I became a licensed Clinical Laboratory Scientist. My professional dream had come true. I loved the work; I loved living on the seashore, having moved to a new home in Newport Beach. Life was good, but I wanted more. I wanted adventure. I wanted to be sophisticated. I wanted to be worldly.

Travel could give me those attributes. I worked extra shifts and sometimes double shifts to augment my savings account. In the summer of 1971, at twenty-five years of age, I set off alone to travel through Europe. None of my friends had the money or the desire to go but that didn't stop me. Frommer's *Europe on Five Dollars a Day* claimed one could travel cheaply. I could travel for several months. I packed up my stuff and said goodbye to my family and friends. Passport and Eurail Pass in hand, International Hostel card and fake student ID in my wallet, I took my first transatlantic flight.

After six weeks of travel, I was tired and lonely. I had seen the significant sites in eight countries—fiords in Norway, canals in Amsterdam, the London Bridge. It was overwhelming. International travel is an education! History came alive, geography was more than a map, and math skills were needed to convert currencies and exchange rates. I had to figure out train schedules in foreign languages. Sometimes I was not sure what I was eating. Every minute was an adventure. But I needed to process what I had learned—study the history of the places I had been, reflect on the beauty of mountains and valleys, and ponder the differences and similarities of various cultures. I returned to Southern California and started working again.

Soon I regretted my decision to return home. There was so much more to see. I began saving my money and planning the next adventure—something I have been doing since that first trip.

The following winter, I skied in Austria for a month. At that time everything cost less in Europe than it did at home. When the snow started melting, like a bird migrating south for warmer weather, I headed to Greece in time for Easter. After visiting the islands, I traveled north to Italy, France, and Germany as spring brought more tourists and sunny skies.

I ended my trip in London, the last stop after a four-month journey. It was there I met King Tutankhamun, the catalyst for my future travel outside the western world. Fifty years after the discovery of King Tut's burial chamber, the Egyptian Museum lent fifty items from his tomb to the British Museum. Posters were plastered on the red double-decker buses and in the London Underground. Announcements of this extraordinary exhibit bombarded me. Visitors from around the world came to London to see the exhibition—the gold, the jewels, the statues.

Late afternoon on my last day in London, I decided to check out those treasures. When I saw the number of people waiting outside the museum, a line that snaked around the building, I almost changed my mind. Placards along the route announced how long the wait would be. Trying to find the end of the line, I passed the one-hour sign, then the two-hour sign. How long was I willing to wait? Today was my only chance. The end of the line was just past the two-and-a-half-hour sign. It was drizzling rain. How wet would I get? How much standing would I endure? I waited.

Finally, I was in the museum. The brilliance of the gold dazzled me. The magnificence of ancient history took root in my consciousness. Artists created these treasures over three thousand years ago! My country is young—not quite two hundred years old. And yet, here I was looking at these ancient objects—so perfect and unchanged. Wonder and awe filled my heart. My mind raced. I must go to Egypt. I resolved to visit King Tut's tomb, the source of these riches.

Security guards urged us onward. Keep moving — no time to stand and gawk.

CRØ

Three years later, in 1975, at the age of twenty-nine, I began my trip around the world. I had nothing to hold me back. No house, no husband or serious boyfriend. I was free and eager for adventure. I was fearless and naïve. The treasures of Egypt and the animals in East Africa were calling me. Little did I know the happiness and sorrow that awaited me on this trip.

When asked how I back-packed around the globe and lived in Africa for over a decade, I reflect on the pictures in *National Geographic*. They opened doors and created mysteries for me. And yet, I did not find an answer to my question—how can people be so different? I found we are more alike than different. We all want to love and be loved, to be seen for who we are, to find happiness, and to live our lives fully. I found kids laughing and playing, curious and shy. Everywhere I visited, I found parents who wanted a better life for their children. I saw people with dignity regardless of education, willing to share what little they had, hard-working, helpful, loving, and kind. I found myself to be a member of the human family and not unlike most people in the world.

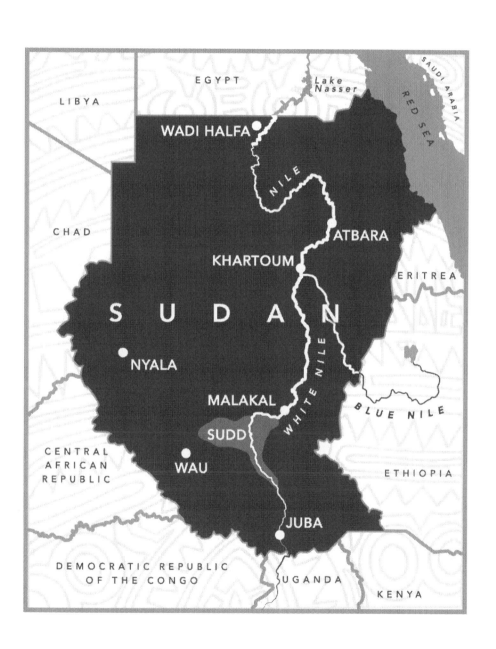

Part One

1975-1988

Pineapples to Pyramids

1975–1976

It must have been the pineapple swimming in its own juice—along with millions of microbes. With my fingers, as countless others had done, I fished out a slice from the tin washtub sitting in the shade of a towering tropical tree. I paid the brightly dressed woman squatting beside the tub. The sweet, juicy fruit—my first taste of Africa—came from the fields surrounding the Nairobi Central Bus Station.

It was December 1975. I had landed that morning at the Jomo Kenyatta International Airport in Kenya. My childhood dream was about to become a reality. I would go on safari to see the animals in East Africa. I was waiting for a bus to take me to Thika, a town twenty-five miles northeast of Nairobi.

In August, five months earlier, I had set off from my home in Palo Alto, CA, to travel around the world. I spent the first month scuba diving at a Club Med in Palinuro on the southwest coast of Italy. The previous April, I had met a Belgian scuba diver working at a Club Med in the Caribbean; I thought I was in love. He was now at the club in Palinuro and soon would go to the club on the Red Sea. After I left the club, I traveled the next few months around the Mediterranean: Sicily, Tunisia, Morocco, and Israel. There was no room at any inn in Jerusalem at Christmas time; so, I flew south of the equator to Africa.

Why do they call it the trots when it's a mad dash to the toilet? It must have been that pineapple! I had checked into a small guest house in Thika. The shared bathroom facility was located in the middle of the locked compound. Five times during the night, I hastily trotted off to the toilet. Fortunately, no one else needed the facility when I did.

Within a few hours of arriving on the continent, my intestinal flora became African.

The next morning, with no lingering effects other than dehydration and loss of sleep, I waited for Nancy Rainbow to pick me up. A friend of mine had met Nancy and her husband several years earlier while traveling in East Africa. Nancy and I had corresponded before I left California; and, she had invited me to stay with her on her coffee farm near Thika.

In the 1950s and 60s, the wild African animals were being hunted to extinction. The catchphrase "shoot the remaining animals with a camera" became a worldwide plea to save these wild creatures. I wanted to go on safari to see the herds before they disappeared. Nancy said she would help me find something suitable. I was in the heart of Africa. My fantasy of seeing these animals in the wild was about to come true.

Nancy Strange was born in England in the early 1900s and immigrated to Kenya as a baby. Her parents started a pig farm. She loved to share stories of her life growing up in the Great Rift Valley of Kenya—giraffes and zebras strolled through the farm, monkeys and parrots were her pets. She married into a family of coffee farmers. She laughed, recalling the newspaper headlines when she and her sister married brothers: "The Strange Girls marry Rainbow Boys." Short and thick in the middle, Nancy appeared to be in her middle sixties. She wore frumpy house dresses and sensible shoes. Her infectious giggle showed her good nature.

Due to the high rate of crime in the country, Nancy did not drive at night. She had recommended that I stay that first night in a guest house close to where the bus stopped. Nancy lived in the master house at Greystone Farm, a coffee plantation she and her husband had planted. When her husband died, several years before my visit, she sold the entire farm to the neighboring village farmers and now rented the house from the villagers. The old plantation house, located in the middle of the fields, was off the grid. Constructed of grey granite stones found in the area, the thick walls of the house provided good insulation from the heat of the African sun. We were south of the equator; it was summer in December.

In the chilly mornings on the farm, I watched the equatorial sunrise over the coffee bushes. That sun would exhaust us with oppressive heat in the afternoon. Occasionally a rain brought cooling breezes. November and December marked the season of the short rains, but they had not come as expected. East Africa was experiencing a severe drought.

Nancy justified growing a few flowers around the house because she sprinkled them with water salvaged from weekly baths. She instructed me to fill the tub with a few inches of water and to use only a little soap. Afterward, we scooped up the precious liquid for her floral garden.

Her kitchen sink drained into a cement groove outside the house into the chicken run. The hens came running when they heard the splash of dishwater—eagerly consuming both the water and the bits of food from our plates. A kerosene refrigerator kept our food cold; I never did understand how heat could create cold. A small diesel generator provided light in the evenings and power for the "wireless" tuned to BBC keeping us informed of world events.

Mungai, Nancy's Kikuyu house servant who lived in a hut inside our compound walls, taught me greetings in Swahili. Every evening, the sound of African drums flowed from the village, serenading me to sleep. At night the watchman arrived in his floor-length, greatcoat, a feather in his felt hat. He sat on top of our compound wall—bow and arrows slung on his back—guarding us while we slept.

Three nights after my arrival (December 22, I will never forget as it's my brother's birthday), I awoke to the shrill sound of a whistle, the shuffling of many feet, and mumbled voices. I thought someone in the village was ill as Nancy had a few pharmacy supplies in her home;

everyday villagers had come to the kitchen window to obtain aspirin or Band-Aids. Soon the scuffles became pounding footsteps, and the mumbled voices became shouts. Angry cries broke the calm of the night. The ear-piercing blare of an air horn startled me; something was wrong. I quickly got out of bed, pulled back the bedcovers, and dove under the bed. Maybe whoever was in the house would think the room was empty.

Soon I saw two dirty, calloused black feet near my bed. Flashlight beams danced around the room. The feet departed. I heard Nancy yelling in pain and anger as two sets of bare feet and flashlight beams again appeared in my room. I heard someone ravage through my backpack then someone peered under the bed. Eye to eye, he violently yanked me from under the bed. The scuba diving watch glittering on my wrist caught his attention. He grabbed my arm, snatched my watch, and jerked me into an arm lock.

"Hey, what are you doing? You're hurting me." I pleaded.

Dragging and pushing me outside while whipping my thighs with a stick, he stopped at the pantry to pick up a knife—a razor-sharp knife Nancy used to cut meat for her cat.

Arm twisted behind my back.

Alcohol breath.

Sharp knife under my chin

Uneven terrain.

What if he stumbles?

Should I resist?

Nancy, what should I do? I thought.

Thrown to the rough ground.

Penetration.

Calm disassociation.

Other men waiting their turn.

Where's the knife?

Can I reach it?

Could I hurt him?
Shouting.
Departing.
"Your friends are leaving," I whispered to him.
He followed them.
They are gone.
Alive!
Where is Nancy?

A gang of five thieves had come through the coffee farm to rob and attack us. One wielded a panga (a wooden club with leather strips knotted at the end) that he used on Nancy's hands as she sounded the air horn. The others had cut branches from the coffee bushes which they split at the end. These switches made the V-shaped welts on my thighs. The thugs had searched the house, knocked Christmas gifts to the floor, demanded that Nancy open the safe and give them the keys to the Land Rover outside in a shed. The safe was empty. The Land Rover belonged to the village; Nancy did not have the keys. The attackers stole a few things, including my camera, stormed out of the house, and ran off through the fields.

I found Nancy in her bedroom with bloody wounds on her head and hands. She asked me, "Did they...?"

"Yes," I replied in a shaky voice, "but I'm okay; I'm not hurt."

She cried. We comforted each other. Am I a coward? Should I have fought back? Did I let this happen?

Nancy's hands were bleeding; her hair was matted with blood. I needed to take care of her. We found alcohol and bandages; I helped clean her wounds. Fortunately, she was not severely hurt. We went outside the house and sat in the rocking chairs on the porch inside the compound. Soon we heard a vehicle leave.

"That sounds like the Land Rover. I hope someone in the village is going for help," Nancy said.

The phone line had been cut. The generator had been disabled. We sat in the dark. Calm and rational during the attack, now I shook. I was scared. I was in shock. I worried they would return. I wanted to run away. I felt dirty.

I wanted to climb the walls of the compound and run into the fields. I felt vulnerable. Nancy said if the attackers found us running away, they might kill us. So we sat, wondering why neither Mungai, the house servant, nor the night watchman, nor the villagers came to our aid.

After half an hour, we got up enough courage to go to the compound gate. Upon opening it, we saw dozens of villagers standing outside, fear on their faces. They cheered when they saw us. We were alive. The villagers feared us dead. Their superstitions about seeing dead people were so ingrained no one dared to be the one to find us. Mungai had been tied up and gagged in his quarters. Fortunately, he wasn't hurt. The nightwatchman claimed he saw twenty-five or thirty men with spears and knives, and, fearing for his life, he had jumped off the wall and run to the village.

Soon the village chief and his sons returned in the Land Rover, bringing the police with them. They fixed the generator, so we had lights to assess the damage. An investigation ensued. The police stole some things, including several wrapped Christmas gifts. Evidence of the attack? They also took the razor-sharp knife. Our physical wounds did not need medical attention; the village chief left to drive the police back to their station.

Now alone, Nancy and I pondered the "if onlys" and "whys" when such bad things happen. She said I could have been seriously injured or killed if I had been British. My American accent had saved me. Many Kenyans were still upset at the British due to the harsh colonial rule of the past. Nancy had lived without harm through eight years of the Mau Mau uprising for independence in the 1950s. She was devastated that we were victims of a different kind of conflict.

Educated, unemployed, hungry young men were turning to theft and violence all over the country.

We left Greystone the next day and spent a solemn Christmas at her sister's home in Karen, a suburb of Nairobi.

The Big Five

"I know where you can find a safari that won't cost so much. Most people arrive from Europe on a prearranged package tour. I hate to think how much that costs," said Nancy. "There's a traveler's bulletin board at the New Stanley. I'm sure we can find something there. And, it will cost about half of what a travel agency in Nairobi would charge."

After Christmas, Nancy took me to the New Stanley Hotel in Nairobi. Named after Henry Morton Stanley of *Dr. Livingston, I presume?*, the hotel was built in the early 1900s and was the traditional meeting place for backpackers traveling in Africa.

How fortunate to know someone who knew the ropes about sightseeing in Kenya. She was right. The bulletin board contained dozens of posts for travel in East Africa.

I was still determined to see the Africa Big Five game animals—lions, leopard, rhinoceros, elephant, and Cape buffalo. I would not let several angry thieves stop me. The bruises on my legs remained, reminding me of the attack, but I pushed fear and negative emotions away. Though my camera and wristwatch had been stolen, my courage and determination persisted, my dignity and self-respect were as strong as ever.

On the bulletin board, I found a notice from Roland, a British citizen visiting Kenya. He had a Land Rover and was looking for five travelers to share expenses on a safari in Kenya and Tanzania. I can't remember how we set it up without Facebook, but four others had also responded to the message, all young American men.

On New Year's Day 1976, we pooled our money and bought fruits and vegetables at the Nairobi City Market and other supplies for our camping safari. Sufficiently stocked, we set out in the afternoon, heading north, our hearts full of delight and anticipation of the adventures to come. I was having fun; the terrible memories of December 22 were fading.

The first stop was Lake Nakuru, home to thousands of flamingos. Masses of the long-necked, red-legged birds covered the shores of the lake. Clattering and squawking, we heard them long before we saw them. Combing the water with their beaks, heads upside down, the elegant birds gracefully filtered the riches from the lake; algae, crustaceans, seeds, and plankton. For some, it was nap time, with head under a wing and standing on one leg; they looked like balls of cotton candy on a broomstick. When startled, the birds filled the sky with coral-pink clouds.

We set up camp near the lake and had our dinner as the sun set. Around the campfire that first night, the discussion turned to travel, especially traveling alone and specifically about women traveling alone. I'm a private person; however, I told my story about the attack at Greystone Farm. Mark, a professional whitewater rafter who had recently completed a trip down the Zambezi River, started with "If that happened to my girlfriend..."

I stopped him. "You think a woman needs your protection? Would you have fought off five strong men to save my honor? I knew there would be risks traveling here. But I am willing to endure the potential hazards to do what I'm doing right now, sitting by a campfire in the heart of Africa. This woman can take care of herself. Do you have a girlfriend who can't take care of herself?"

That precipitated a lively but levelheaded discussion about men, women, rape, travel, fear, and courage. The exchange with these men my age confirmed my resolve to continue my trip around the world.

11

We had started that day as strangers, and already we had become close friends. Openness, trust, and respect would seal those friendships.

Time for bed. One two-person tent, five guys and one gal. I accepted the offer to sleep in the tent every night. The fellows would rotate through the tent while the others slept under the stars of the African night. Roland slept in his Land Rover. Either for his safety or the security of the vehicle—I never did figure that out. I would share my sleeping quarters with a different young man every night.

Nevertheless, the men were respectful. The fellows were open-minded. These young Americans knew the new societal rules established in the sixties. They did not expect me to cook and wash up at every meal nor to engage in sex—unless I wanted to do so. I have to admit there was one special guy. I was happy and satisfied when it was his turn to sleep in the tent. Did anyone else know? No one seemed to care what went on in my tent.

The next day we headed to the Masai Mara reserve, a sea of grass and low shrub as far as we could see. In the far distance, we could barely discern the hills and escarpment to the west and the Mountains of the Moon to the northeast. We drove through the savanna following the countless herds of wildebeest, zebra, and gazelle grazing as they marched north to greener pastures. They were unconcerned by our presence. We camped in the park under the acacia trees that dotted the landscape. The crisp blue sky, awash in cotton-ball clouds, extended from one distant horizon to the other. Masai Mara becomes the plains of the Serengeti when crossing the border from Kenya into Tanzania. We had to show our passports at the checkpoint between the two countries; the animals continued their migration unhindered.

The dry rock ravines in the Olduvai Gorge revealed little to me of how our stone tool-using ancestors lived. Gone were the tools; gone were Louis and Mary Leakey. Gone were the archaeology students who toiled under the hot African sun. I was left to wonder about humanity and our progress in the last 1.8 million years. When did we separate ourselves from our environment, Is my modern life an improvement? And how in the world did anyone find this place, so remote, so desolate?

Ngorongoro Crater, an inactive volcanic caldera measuring twelve miles across, is unique among animal preserves. The hillsides of the volcano are so steep the animals spend their entire life inside the crater. Humans too had limited access; therefore, tribal hunters and poachers rarely visited. Fortunately, we had the required four-wheel-drive transport, or we would not have been allowed into the park. In this controlled environment, the animals were unafraid of vehicles; we drove close to the grazing herds. Signposts reminded us the animals were wild; so, we stayed inside our Land Rover—most of the time. In a designated area, we got out of the vehicle and ate our picnic lunch while curious monkeys eyed us from the trees close by, hoping to steal a morsel of food. We were not allowed to camp in the crater, so we left before nightfall. We set up camp just outside the park. I was alarmed by the sound of snuffling and snorting when I awoke during the night. I was in a tent in the middle of the African plains! My heart pounded. Given a choice, I would rather be attacked by a wild animal than a fellow human being. The following morning I awoke thinking about the animals that were as curious about me as I was of them.

The next day we drove through Lake Manyara National Park, famous for lions reclining on tree branches. Although Roland drove slowly through the park, no one spotted the king of beasts in a tree. Birds and monkeys studied us from the trees. Browsers trimmed the tree branches not far off the road. Elephants trumpeted at us, and rhinos skeptically regarded us. Thousands of flamingos honked and screeched on the lakeshore. Possibly leopards peered at us from under the brush. Aren't they night hunters? I hope I don't see two golden eyes peering into the tent tonight. I was glad I would not be sleeping under the stars.

We spent the next night in a guest house in Arusha. We had a shower and slept in a bed, our first shower and first bed since leaving Nairobi six days earlier. The modest guest house felt luxurious.

In the morning, we drove to the town of Moshi. Walking to find a place for breakfast, I rounded a corner on the main street. I stopped in my tracks! There, at the end of the road, I had my first sight of the highest peak in Africa—Kilimanjaro. A clear day with an unobstructed view—postcard perfect. We were fortunate because clouds usually obscure the top of the mountain. Standing at over 19,000 feet, the volcanic massif is so high it creates its own weather system. This spectacular mountain stands alone. No foothills or other highland peaks steal the view of the majestic snow-capped mountain on the flat, dry savanna. The next day we continued our trip from Moshi for a closer look at Kilimanjaro.

Leaving the savanna and animals behind, we headed southwest to the coastal town of Tanga on the Indian Ocean. Palm trees and sand, a fleet of wooden fishing boats bobbing not far from shore. However, so many youngsters hassled us on the beach that we left the next day to the quiet village of Moa.

There we made camp on the sugar-white beach at the edge of the ocean. The village elders helped us prepare our dinner of skewered fish on sticks cooked over an open fire. We spent two relaxing days drinking cold beer and eating hot pizza. I felt like I was in a National Geographic photo. A tropical paradise, a lovely place if one ignored the smell of human waste wafting down the beach.

We left Tanzania and drove north along the coast to the port town of Mombasa in Kenya. After a thousand years, the city is still an important center for trade in spices, gold, and ivory with Asia and the Arab world. We visited a Portuguese fort and walked the narrow, twisting streets of the old town. We replenished our supplies and spent another night in a guest house. After one last swim in the tropical waters, we headed to our final game park.

Tsavo East National Park was severely affected by the drought in East Africa. The elephants were so hungry they had pushed trees to the ground to eat the leaves. Dead trees and dead elephants littered the park. We could smell putrid, rotten elephant carcasses in various stages of decomposition long before we saw them. We examined one of the many elephant skeletons along the roadside, the enormous bones having been scattered by the survivors of the herd. The death of so many trees impacted the birds, monkeys, and other animals. Droughts and floods, grasses and trees, animal species large and small, interdependent cycles in the circle of life.

After two glorious weeks—a time of reflection, a time of healing, a time of forgetting—we arrived in Nairobi, hot, sweaty, and exhausted. We parted with hugs and promised to keep in touch, grateful for our memorable experiences and solid new friendships. We did not stay in touch, but the memories are still with me.

Images I won't forget:

· The giant burnt-orange sun setting behind acacia trees.

· Mama elephant trumpeting "get out of here" as we limped off with a flat tire.

· The sound of sucking mud as a rhino slowly pulled out of his mud bath, turning a watchful eye on us.

· The elegant king of the beasts relaxing, his cubs scrambled over his body.

· The Cape buffalo, robust as tanks, glaring at us, ready to charge, daring us to come closer.

· Grunts, groans, and rustling leaves, the alarming night sounds as we sat around our campfire.

We had seen four of the African Big Five: elephants, rhinoceros, Cape buffalo, and lions. Leopards eluded us.

CRISO

Thirty years later, I visited South Luangwa National Park in Zambia with my second husband, Jim. During our five day stay, we saw leopards every day; leopards in the daytime, leopards in the evening, leopards sleeping in trees—their legs dangling below the branches, leopards doing a full cat stretch before jumping to another limb. I witnessed a leopard racing across the dirt track in front of our open vehicle. Two curious leopard kittens stared at us from under the bushes on the side of the road.

One evening after dinner, a park scout escorted Jim and me back to our bungalow. He swept the area along the path with the beam of a spotlight, watching for danger. Suddenly he froze and whispered, "Stop, don't move." He had spotted an animal with spots. There, in the beam of light, thirty feet away, was a full-grown leopard drinking from a puddle in front of our cottage. The big cat casually turned his head to look us in the eye. My heart was racing. How fast can he run? How fast can I run? How far can he jump? Is he hungry? He was not impressed. He looked away and continued his lapping. The alarm-shrieks of nearby impalas filled the air. We slowly proceeded to our front door as the scout watched the big cat. Once inside, we were instructed to lock the door and stay inside. However, we monitored the leopard through our screen door, and soon he slowly sauntered off into the African bush.

My count was now complete. I had seen all of the African Big Five in the wild.

Falling in Love

1976

"Why do you want to go to Sudan?" asked the consular service officer representing Sudan at the British Embassy in Nairobi. Smirking like he was talking to a child, he continued, "There's no border crossing between Sudan and Kenya. And the border between Uganda and Sudan is also closed."

"I don't want to go to Sudan. I am traveling to Egypt, and Sudan lies between here and there," I responded.

Dressed in his impeccable business suit, he retorted, "Oh, you're a backpacker? You know traveling like this can be dangerous."

Little did he know what I had already been through. I wondered if he had ever been to Sudan or even outside his diplomatic circle in Nairobi. I knew about the border closures. Can he deny me a visa? I hadn't considered that possibility; I usually get what I want. Was he trying to discourage me? What would be my backup plan?

"I plan to fly to Juba in the south of Sudan then travel overland from there to Egypt," I replied.

I guess he could see my determination and realized I was not a novice traveler. He granted the visa.

While I was waiting for my visa interview, I had met two Australian nurses, Laura and Hilary, who were also at the embassy to get visas for Sudan.

"How did it go?" Laura asked as I left the consular office.

"It wasn't automatically granted, but I did get my visa. Let him know you are veteran travelers. I'll see you in Juba," I answered.

During the past year, Laura and Hilary, also in their late twenties, had traveled overland from South Africa and were on their way to Egypt via Sudan. Traveling on even less than my shoe-string budget, Laura and Hilary planned to take a bus from Nairobi to Kampala, the capital of Uganda. There they would catch another bus as far north as they could, then figure out what to do. They invited me to go with them, but the attack on the coffee farm was too fresh in my mind. I wasn't up for that kind of travel. Idi Amin was the president of Uganda at the time. There was much tension within Uganda, with its neighbors, and with most of the world. I thought it best to avoid that country. I bought an airline ticket from Nairobi to Juba.

We had worked out a plan to meet up at the Juba youth hostel where I intended to stay. Laura and Hilary were going to camp behind the police station as they heard it was both free and safe.

My flight from Nairobi to Juba on Sudan Airlines went without incident. However, when I picked up my backpack, I discovered the shoulder strap had been ripped off at one end. As Sudan Airlines was an international carrier, I expected them to repair the damage. Sometimes events happen that change the course of one's life. This incident was such an event. Little did I know Sudan would become my home for the next twelve years.

The young men working in the Sudan Airways office in Juba were from the capital city, Khartoum. Probably they had never had a request for luggage repair.

Smartly dressed in his uniform, Osman examined the strap and asked, "What do you want us to do?"

Annoyed, I said, "I expect you to fix my backpack. I can't carry it without both straps."

Taking a closer look, Hassan asked: "Do you think sewing it would make it strong enough?"

I supposed it was worth a try. The young men closed the office, and we set out to find a tailor. With me in the prized passenger seat, the others piled into the back of their official pickup truck, and Babiker drove through town in search of a tailor.

I was shocked to see that although Juba was a large city by population, it was little more than an overgrown village. There were two miles of paved roads, one hotel, and the youth hostel. Very few homes or businesses had electricity or running water. Women wrapped in colorful garb, balancing food, water, or household goods, on their heads, lined the roads. Poverty for sure. Maybe the British consul was right when he tried to discourage me from visiting Sudan.

Soon we pulled up under the shade of a large tree. In the dirt under the shady canopy was an old man with an even older sewing machine. I understood not a word of the conversation, but the round-faced man in his dirty *jelabiya* took my backpack and, bare feet on the treadle, got to work. He reattached the strap to my pack. I slipped the straps over my shoulders; the repair felt strong. A smile was the only payment the tailor would accept.

"Where are you going to stay? We'll drop you off," asked Hassan. "You know the Juba Hotel is full."

"Oh, I'm staying at the youth hostel. I'm meeting a couple of friends there." I said, not wanting them to think I was alone.

"Not a good idea," stated Osman. "The hostel is dirty, and there is funny business going on there. Some of the people are not very nice."

Interestingly, the youth hostel in Juba was probably the only one in the world that charged more for a bed outside than inside. Sleeping on a cot under the trees, cooled by the occasional breeze, was preferable to the hot, stuffy rooms inside.

They invited me to stay at the Sudan Airways rest house where they lived while stationed in Juba. I told them about my new friends, Laura and Hilary, and that they would be camping behind the police station. They said their rest house was walking distance to the police station. Anyway, they said I needed to register with the police so we would check tomorrow and leave a message for my friends if they were not yet there. The fellows were friendly, helpful, and polite. I felt I would be safe with them, probably safer than at the hostel.

The Sudan Airways rest house was a two-story concrete building with six bedrooms, a kitchen, and two shower rooms. Although it was plain, without paint or curtains, it was clean, and it was the nicest building I had seen so far in Juba. Osman and Hassan doubled up so I could have my own private room. It was pleasant; there was electricity most of the time and warm water for showers. A cook provided three meals a day. I enjoyed the company of the young Sudanese men. In the afternoons after work, Osman and the cook taught me Arabic. Soon I was greeting people in their language and knew the names of many foods.

The toilet was a wooden outhouse, smelling-distance away from the rest house. There were three small cubicles, each with a wooden door for privacy. I've seen plenty of outhouses in my life, but this one surprised me. Inside, in the middle of a wooden board, was a round hole, hand-cut by the looks of it. I sure hoped I wouldn't get splinters in a most delicate place. On the floor was a plastic bucket full of clean water—I assumed it was clean—with a red plastic cup floating on top. Knowing this is how much of the world cleans the private parts, I was glad I had brought toilet paper. Directly beneath the hole, on the ground, was a battered tin bucket next to a small trapdoor on the back of the structure. It never occurred to me what happened when the bucket was full. Imagine my surprise one morning when I was sitting on the hole and felt a gust of warm air coming from below. I looked down and saw a long black arm reaching in for the bucket. A night-soil collector had opened the back flap and was removing my bucket in mid-stream! I wonder if that man tells the story of seeing a tender white rump through the hole. After that, I always checked to see if the donkey-powered honey wagon was coming down the road before I used the facilities.

A few days after I arrived in Juba, Laura and Hilary arrived at the police station.

"Hey, you made it!" I was happy to see my friends, the only other Caucasian people I had seen up to this point.

"Boy, you should be glad you flew here. Our trip was the worst since we left home," exclaimed Hilary. On the chubby side, she was breathing hard from the short walk we were taking

Laura added, "We had to walk across the border. It was brutal. We were in a group of a dozen Africans, and none of them spoke English." Tall and fit, she appeared to have come through the ordeal unscathed.

"When our bus out of Kampala reached its final destination, we caught a ride in the back of a cargo truck. The truck was not allowed to cross the border between Uganda and Sudan. Everyone had to get out. We walked for several miles, carrying all our possessions. I guess we crossed the border at some point. Finally, we caught another truck that brought us here to Juba."

After hearing their story, I was glad I had taken the quick flight from Nairobi.

Laura, Hilary, and I intended to catch the mail boat going north on the Nile River towards Khartoum. Juba was the southern end of the line for mail delivery in Sudan. No roads or railroads connected the north with the south. The mail was transported by boat along the White Nile. The boat took a few passengers as it delivered letters at various stops on the river between Kosti and Juba. However, without a set schedule, one never knew when it would arrive. There was no other public transportation out of Juba except by air, and the ticket to Khartoum was expensive. Laura, Hilary, and I planned to wait in Juba until the boat arrived and then head north with the mail. The trip could take about a week, and we would need to bring our food, water, and bedding. Laura and Hilary had their camping gear; I hoped I could find a blanket somewhere. I dreaded the expected hardship, the boredom, the heat, and the bugs, but I was up to the challenge and the adventure. I knew it would be quite a story—after it was over. The boat would meander on the river through the Sudd, the world's most extensive wetlands that surround the White Nile. Eager to be on our way north, we checked the post office every day to see if they knew when the boat would arrive.

During our stay in Juba, we met every day, played cards, read books, and explored the town. In the evenings, the rest house became a meeting place for many young men from Khartoum working in Juba. Laura and Hilary joined in the fun. We talked, we laughed, we danced to popular Western music; Abba sang "Waterloo," and Eric Clapton shot the sheriff, but he did not shoot the deputy. The young men were polite, respectful, and loved their home city of Khartoum.

"Khartoum is so much nicer than Juba. You will love it there. We have a cinema and a museum. The sweet juicy watermelons are this big," extending their arms like one telling a fish story about the one that got away. "The grapefruits are as big as soccer balls and sweet as honey. You can buy anything you want in Khartoum." Each young man added a testimony regarding the wonders available in Khartoum.

My stay was pleasant. I felt safe and pampered. I appreciated the opportunity to get to know the Sudanese people. Nationalities were irrelevant; we were young people having a good time.

However, the thoughts of my hosts must have been very different. What a shock it was when Hassan proposed marriage. How did he see me? A young woman traveling alone, did he think I needed protection? Did he sense loneliness? Was he trying to save me from becoming a spinster? After all, I was twenty-nine years old. In his culture, women marry in their teens. Men marry when they have saved enough money for a wedding and a bride, usually when they are in their thirties. Hassan and I had slow danced a few times. Did that signal a desire to

22

spend the rest of my life with him? How different dating must be in his culture. I politely refused. My travel plans were most important to me.

That was the first of three marriage proposals I got that month; I accepted the third one.

A week after I arrived in Juba, Ahmed, a middle-aged man who was a Sudan Airways manager from Khartoum, came to stay at the rest house. He arrived in a small plane piloted by Captain Sukkar, hired from an air taxi service in Khartoum. Ahmed's job was to survey the dirt landing strips in the area. After spending an evening with us— Laura, Hilary, and me—Ahmed offered to fly us to Khartoum with him when he completed his work. We were ready to go. One week in Juba was enough. A flight sure sounded better than sleeping on the deck of a boat. We eagerly accepted his offer, hoping it was genuine.

Two days later, Ahmed returned to the rest house and announced Captain Sukkar was ready to leave. I quickly packed up and said my hasty good-byes. We picked up Laura and Hilary on the way to the airport. Driving to the airport, Ahmed told us about the beautiful places we could visit in Khartoum where he lived with his mother and extended family.

Ahmed said, looking directly at me, "Why don't you come home with me during your stay in Khartoum? We have a big house. I'll show you around the city. And who knows, maybe we will get married someday."

What? Another shock! What is it with these guys? Are there no Sudanese women to marry? What did this free air travel entail? What would be the real price or the expectation? We were three women and two men; still, the offer of the free flight seemed like a good idea.

At the airport, we saw the bright orange-red, single-engine plane. An angry, young, longish-haired blond guy in blue shirt and tan shorts was stomping around the plane, kicking the tires of the aircraft. Through the open windows of the car, we could hear him swearing loudly in French, "*Putain de merde*," and punctuating the air with a heavily-accented "fuckin cunt."

"You're late. We should have taken off two hours ago." He stopped yelling when he saw three young white women get out of the car with Ahmed and Captain Sukkar.

When introduced to this loud-mouthed guy, I asked, "Who are you?"

"ME? I'M THE PILOT!" he shouted,

Thus, in February 1976, I met my future ex-husband, Daniel Van der Smissen. A few weeks later, he would also propose marriage. I was twenty-nine years old, never engaged, and now I had a choice of husbands.

Captain Daniel was upset because they were scheduled to take off at 7 a.m. It was now after 9 a.m. It turned out Captain Sukkar was the co-pilot. After a few remarks about hot air currents and plane crashes, we were airborne. Daniel and Sukkar sat in the front seats flying the plane, Ahmed and I sat in the middle, Laura and Hilary took the rear seats.

We flew low over the Sudd. What joy to cruise above the wetlands. Many small islands dotted the shallow water. We saw a few mud and grass huts built on the larger ones. People walked on raised pathways between the islands, dug-out canoes glided smoothly through the water, trees rose majestically from the swamp, and birds soared on gentle currents. For over an hour, we marveled at this wetland stretching as far as the eye could see. What a tedious voyage it would have been on the mail boat.

Eventually, the wetlands gave way to the dry, flat bushland of the savannas. The White Nile once again emerged as a river near the town of Malakal, our destination for the night. A van and driver were waiting for us when we landed at the airport. After a few miles on a bumpy dirt road, we arrived at a rest house where we would spend the night.

Daniel: "What are you doing in Sudan?"

Me: "Traveling from Kenya to Egypt."

D: "Where are you from?"

M: "California, and you?"

D: "I'm Belgian."

Oh boy! My last lover was a Belgian. After meeting him again at the Club Med in Eilat, Israel, I realized he was not the man for me. I had left him for good when I departed for Kenya. He was fun, a great dancer, but I realized we had no future together. Hmm...another Belgian?

Four empty rooms in the rest house, six people from the plane. The sleeping arrangements were made after dinner, after drinks, after funny cigarettes, after much conversation and laughter, after a few passionate kisses in the moonlight.

Many years later, Daniel recalled to our daughter, "Your mother was not shy."

When I met him, Daniel had been in Sudan for three months and was ready to leave. Flying for Khalil's Air Taxi was a step up from his previous jobs as a crop dusting pilot in several African countries. But Sudan, a hot, dry, Muslim country, was very different from the lively French-speaking countries of Morocco, Madagascar, and Zaire where he had previously worked. Thirty-five-years-old, he proudly stated that he had lived in Africa for fifteen years *sans chapeau* (without a hat), and that is why he was so *fou* (crazy). Now here comes this young, adventurous, educated, liberated American woman out of the jungle who would change his life.

The next day I sat in the co-pilot's seat. Sukkar sat in the back with Laura and Hilary. As we flew over the savanna on our way to Khartoum, the airplane startled wild animals below us: antelope bounced in herd formation, elephant lumbered away from the noise, giraffe stopped eating ready to take flight, and other small grazers scattered in the grass. As we got closer to Khartoum, the savanna gave way to the desert. Through this barren landscape flowed the White Nile with a ribbon of green on each side, the crops sustaining the lives of people and animals alike. When we landed in Khartoum, I went home with Daniel to his company's rest house; Laura and Hilary went home with Sukkar. Ahmed went home alone to his mother and extended family.

Daniel was silly and often immature, making the silverware dance at the dinner table. He was precise in his thoughts and opinions. He read books. He loved history, especially the history of Europe and ancient Egypt. He had left home in Brussels at twenty years of age for adventure in the Belgian Congo.

Referring to Belgium, he said, "Small country, small mind."

He needed all of Africa to expand his mind. Africa became his home. He was adventurous, tramping through the jungles as a radio operator; then, as a pilot, landing planes on questionable runways. He told his stories of adventure with humor and self-deprecation. He was generous. He dressed with care. He was fit and healthy. He walked with determination. He drank but never to drunkenness. He missed the dancing and nightclubs prominent in the Francophone African countries. However, with me, he was having fun in Sudan. He didn't want me to leave.

The Air Taxi jet was scheduled to go to Switzerland in two weeks for maintenance. Gunter, a German pilot of the plane, offered us, all three women, a free ride to Cairo, a refueling stop. Hitching by air was an excellent way to bypass the hot, dry, desert. But the jet wasn't ready to fly to Europe two weeks later, so Laura and Hilary headed north to Egypt on the train. During this time, the attraction between Daniel and me developed into a deep romance. I decided to await the free plane ride to Cairo. Two weeks turned into a month, as I soon learned was the usual occurrence in Sudan.

Daniel had no vehicle. He had no place to live. He had a job he didn't like. He had no money in the bank. He had no immediate family except his parents in Belgium. Nevertheless, he had both a Swiss and American Air Line Pilots License giving him the potential for career improvement.

I was the only woman in the rest house for the foreign pilots working for Air Taxi. There was little for me to do, no cleaning, no cooking, no shopping, no TV, no radio. We swam every afternoon at the German Club across the street from our living quarters. Most evenings, we dined on the lawn of the club, under the stars, with several other pilots.

Late one afternoon, ever the romantic, Daniel rented a felucca so we could watch the sunset on the Nile River. I felt so special; we sat close together, holding hands, even though we were the only couple on a boat that could carry more than a dozen people. The skipper navigated the river proficiently, skillfully tacking from one side to the other. We sailed around Tuti Island, where the summer floods drenched the soil with life-giving nutrients. Now, during the winter, the river was peaceful. Farmers irrigated their crops growing on the island by hoisting water in leather buckets tied to long poles. Men fished from the banks. People bathed in the shallow water near the river bank. Women washed clothes in the river then put them over bushes to dry. Goats drank from the river. As the sun set, birds flew to their evening roost. If Daniel was trying to impress me, he succeeded.

Nevertheless, Khartoum was a dry, dusty, dirty town of a million people. I later learned I was there during the best time of the year— the best weather, the best selection of farm produce, and reliable electrical power. Still, resources and supplies were limited. The few shops had half-empty shelves. There was little for me in Khartoum. It was not a place I would choose to live.

We took taxis everywhere we went. The canary yellow vehicles were readily available in neighborhoods and in town. Most people did not have private cars; the local buses overflowed with passengers. I soon found out that old cars never die; they become taxis. Sometimes the doors opened only from inside or only from outside. Mostly the tires were bald. Always the seats were ripped and patched with tape (or not). Often the taxi looked like a crab; the body pointed off-kilter from the wheels. Never did the driver speak English but he was always polite and helpful and managed to get us where we wanted to go.

Finally, six weeks after my arrival in Khartoum, the jet was ready to leave for Switzerland. I would get my free flight to Cairo. However, now, I faced a dilemma. Daniel and I had fallen in love. He wanted me to return to Khartoum.

"Go to Egypt. See the pyramids. But please come back to me. We can get married if you want to. I love you. Come back to Khartoum," he begged.

Why would I come back to such a place? Love? Is that what it was? How can one know for sure? This relationship was different from any other I had experienced. It was exciting. It wasn't the locality; it must be the man. It wasn't passion, but he intrigued me. I had no friends with which to talk this over. What was it about him that captured my interest, captured my heart?

After seven months of living out of a backpack, was travel wearing me down? Was I tired of too much adventure? I am a person who needs to be needed. I felt needed. I felt loved.

I promised to return, to stay for a while, but not necessarily to get married. I was good at being single. But I did want love; I wanted children. I had just celebrated my thirtieth birthday. I had cried. Was I to become an old maid? Maybe it was time. Perhaps Daniel was the one.

Initially, it was my love for Daniel that brought me back. Over time I fell in love with the life we had, the Sudanese people, the opportunities, the excitement, the adventure. My love for this man would soon transform into a deep and abiding love for Africa.

Egypt

1976

The day arrived; the plane was ready to leave Khartoum. I thought of Laura and Hilary as we flew over the broad expanse of the Sahara Desert. I was glad not to be on a train; I liked hitchhiking on airplanes.

Gunther, the pilot, his wife Renee, and I set out from Khartoum early on an April morning. It was spring in Cairo where a drizzle of rain greeted us. Cold rain, not the warm tropical rain I left south of the Equator in East Africa. I was glad I had a jacket with me.

Backpack firmly on my shoulders, good walking shoes on my feet; I was once again a tourist, and once again, a single woman traveling on my own. King Tut had called me from the depth of his tomb. I was in Egypt—his birthplace, his legacy. However, I felt alone. I was lonely. I was a woman in love. Was this the break I needed to assess my future? Would I become a wife soon? Does Daniel miss me? Has he changed his mind? I wished he were with me in Egypt.

Referencing my travel book about North Africa, I hailed a taxi to take me to an inexpensive, safe hotel in the center of Cairo. I left my shoe-string budget behind; I was engaged and would return to Khartoum.

The city was chaos—pedestrians packed the sidewalks, bumping shoulders and other body parts; car horns blared; drivers shouted from their motionless vehicles; one massive traffic jam. Soot–stained buildings reached for the sky, windowpanes so dirty one could not see through them. Electrical wires and phone cables ran from transformers to building after building, looping over the street like a plate of spaghetti. How I longed for the quiet, peaceful streets of Khartoum.

While I was walking to the Egyptian Museum, a young man approached me and flashed open his long coat revealing his family jewels. I turned away and blushed; I supposed that was his intent. How dare he! Had anyone else seen him? He seemed so proud, as well he should have, but that would never have happened in Khartoum.

The Museum of Egyptian Antiquities is one of the most famous in the world. Housing five thousand years of Egyptian history; the collection contains over one hundred thousand items—small as a coin to entire temples. One could spend a lifetime of study there. I had one day. The display cases were dusty, cluttered, and without identification. I wasn't sure what I was seeing.

I walked through the dimly lit corridors and noticed the tour guides had flashlights. I discreetly followed behind a tour so I could catch some of the narratives. Colorful papyrus scrolls, colossal statues twenty-five feet tall, gold and precious stone jewelry, sarcophagi, wooden boats; how can these elaborate items, so well preserved, be thousands of years old? The mummies were both incredible and weird—hair, fingernails, skin. I decided I want to be cremated.

One didn't need a flashlight to view the golden glow from the King Tut collection. The beauty was overwhelming. The gold, the craft, the artistry; I couldn't relate present-day Egypt to the ancient past. And yet, had life in the villages along the Nile changed much from ancient times? Was privileged life so long ago better than life today? My mind filled with questions and wonder—about humanity, about civilization, about the future of my species. Thank you, King Tut, for bringing me here.

Leaving the commotion of the city, I took the public bus to Giza to see the one remaining Seven Wonders of the Ancient World. Soon the tops of the pyramids loomed above the dunes of the desert. Excitement filled me. Then I was there! Me, the gal from a small farming community! Standing at the base of the Egyptian Pyramids! Craning my head back to see the top. No wonder architects still puzzle about how these were built. The size of the stone blocks, the precision of the construction. How was it done so long ago?

I climbed up the sloping, jagged, roughhewn blocks on the face of a pyramid. About one-third of the way up the wall, I entered a small passageway and bumped my head on the low overhang. Following my guide, we climbed up the stone passage inside the tomb. I had to bend over at the waist to avoid hitting the ceiling. Abruptly, the passageway slanted steeply downward. Fortunately, my shoes held their grip on the stone path. After a few minutes, we came to a small chamber with a stone sarcophagus inside. How did it get in there? The air was stuffy. Was it ancient air? From four thousand years ago? The tunnels in the pyramid weren't built with airflow in mind; the dead didn't need fresh air. My thoughts turned to the weight of the stones blocks overhead. I was comforted to think this edifice had been standing for over four thousand years; most likely, it wouldn't collapse while I was inside.

The Great Sphinx reclines near the pyramids. Blending in with the desert sand, the majestic beast stares into the future. Mystery surrounds the origin, the purpose, the builder. Once buried in sand to its shoulders, the first excavation is said to have started 3500 years ago. I am reminded of how trivial we are, how insignificant our time on earth.

After several days in the hustle and bustle of Cairo, I was ready to head south. I took the overnight train to Luxor and awoke refreshed in my sleeper car. I finished my morning tea as the train pulled into the station. I rejoiced in the quiet streets, vendors with trays of bread for sale, and donkeys packed with supplies going to market. This is the Egypt I wanted to see. Although the dusty town was the second most popular destination for travelers, it wasn't yet high season.

The lure in Luxor is the Karnak, also known as the Ancient City of Thebes, the world's largest open-air museum. Constructed over a period of 1500 years, the temple complex is best known for the massive carved columns, over one hundred of them, joined on the top by monolithic beams weighing about seventy tons. I walked among the monoliths picturing the beauty and glory of the bustling ancient city that housed over a million people. The Karnak was built at about the same time as the pyramids, a time frame unfathomable to me. The United States Constitution was ratified two hundred years ago, a blink in the eye of human history.

I crossed the Nile River in a water taxi to catch a public bus to the burial grounds for the kings and queens. The Valley of the Kings contains pharaohs' tombs carved out of the solid rock hillsides. Not far from there lies The Valley of the Queens where the graves of the pharaohs' wives are located. The valleys are desolate—no vegetation, dry, dusty ravines, and hills of solid rock. The surface of the moon must look like this. I was allowed to enter one tomb and marveled at the carved and painted walls of stone. I visited the entrance to King Tut's tomb; however, that day, it was closed to the public. My thoughts raced back to my afternoon at the British Museum, so grateful I had waited for hours in the drizzling rain to see the treasures of King Tut. How could such riches have been sealed into this fortress cut from solid rock in the middle of nowhere so long ago?

From Luxor, I took a train to Aswan, heading south up the Nile. It seems odd to me that the Nile River flows from the Equator, north to the Mediterranean Sea. The weather became warmer, and the clamor of modern life lessened the further south I went. After the spectacular ancient monuments full of tourists in Cairo, Aswan was a pleasant sleepy village; I walked everywhere I needed to go. Cows, donkeys, and camels shared the streets with cars and people. No one seemed to be in a hurry.

I visited the unfinished ancient obelisk cut in a quarry but left in its bed of granite. It gave me insights into the ancient Egyptian stone-working techniques. Marks from the workers' tools were still visible after 3500 years.

Late one afternoon, I hired a small felucca, sails ready, to watch the sun set behind the sand dunes, reflecting red and gold on the Nile River. The boatman expertly sailed around several rocky islands in the calm water of the river. I missed Daniel most at this time, remembering our sailing together the previous month. How wonderful it would have been to share this place with him. After two unforgettable weeks in Egypt, I was eager to head south to Khartoum, to Daniel.

I booked my ticket on the ferry that crosses Lake Nasser. The boat would take me to Wadi Halfa, on the Sudanese/Egyptian border, to meet the train that crosses the Nubian Desert to Khartoum. I sent Daniel a telegram so he would know when to expect me.

On a late afternoon, I made my way to the ferry dock on the lake. Hordes of people were pushing and shoving, babies and chickens in hand, trying to get to the front of the crowd before boarding was allowed. When I saw the ferry, a double-decker wooden boat with a hint of green paint, I wasn't sure I wanted to get aboard. Black smoke poured from the smokestack. Even without passengers, it listed to one side. I'm a good swimmer, but the lake is enormous. I wondered if they had life vests for every passenger.

Suddenly the crowd surged forward. Everyone wanted to stake a claim to the best area on the open deck. In addition to the chickens, every family carried cooking supplies and charcoal braziers. Groups spread out their provisions like it was a picnic. Even before we left the dock, water was boiling for tea. What if the boat catches fire?

The 340 mile trip across Lake Nasser to the Sudanese border would take thirty-six hours. I had booked one of the several cabins, so I didn't need to rush to claim my space. My cabin was about the size of a walk-in closet. The bunk beds had thin cotton mattresses with clean, threadbare sheets. The single chair had splayed legs, probably wouldn't hold a five-year-old child. Standing in the middle of the room, I could touch both sides of the walls. Aren't prison cells larger than this? The door locked from inside and outside. I felt both me and my possessions would be safe. I expected a roommate as the cabin was double occupancy. It would be nice to share the room with a Sudanese or Egyptian woman for the two nights on the ferry. I was disappointed when no one else showed up.

The people in the cabins shared the sinks and toilets. The toilet dumped into the lake. I don't want to think about where the water in the sink came from. My cabin reservation included food; I had nothing to do but relax and enjoy the journey.

It was late afternoon when we began our journey; the lake was calm, the shores were barren. Was this to be the scenery for the next few days? Lake Nasser was still filling up with water after the completion of the Aswan High Dam five years earlier. The rising water had flooded hundreds of villages. I reflected on those communities, the sorrow of the Nubians who were relocated from their homeland, their homeland for thousands of years. Fortunately, with UNESCO's assistance, the impressive ancient ruins of Abu Simbel had been dismantled and reconstructed away from the rising water of the lake.

The days were long—the relentless chug of the engine, the constant smell of diesel, the monotony of the scenery. Thank goodness I was reading *War and Peace*. At over one thousand pages, it should see me through to Khartoum. Meals were the only distraction. Time for breakfast (bread and jam). Read. Time for lunch (tea and beans with bread). Read. Time for dinner (tea and tough meat stew with bread). Before bed, it was time for tea and a dry biscuit. Boring. Monotonous. Repetitive.

Nevertheless, the weather was perfect, clear and warm in the daytime, clear and fresh in the evenings. The lake was smooth as glass. The desert sands met the water's edge; once in a while, one could see a few dunes, a few bushes, and a hill in the distance. However, most of the time, the view was water.

For two nights, the rolling of the ferry lulled me to sleep. On the third day, I awoke to a bright, clear sky, and more bread and jam with my tea. Soon, the ferry would dock. Emigration out of Egypt. Immigration into Sudan. The train bound for Khartoum awaited us. Was my visa in order? I hoped there would be no problem at this border crossing in the middle of the desert, in the middle of nowhere.

I got on the train. Was I on my way to my new home? Was my trip around the world finished? Would I find what I was looking for? Even without knowing what I was looking for? Doubts and excitement filled my soul.

Stuck in the Desert

1976

The train slowed down, then stopped. From the window, I saw a limitless expanse of desert, an expansive vastness of sand, sand, and more sand. Not a tree, bush, or weed anywhere. The red sunset behind the undulating dunes created a mirage of fresh, clear water. April 1976, the United States was preparing for the biggest celebration in 200 years, and I sat on a motionless train in the middle of the Sahara Desert.

We had traveled an hour from the border at Wadi Halfa, heading south to Khartoum. The five hundred sixty mile trip would take twenty-four hours. The setting sun brought relief from the scorching heat of mid-day. People poured from the train, jugs of water and rugs in hand, and began to wash: face and ears, head, arms, legs, then feet. It was time for the evening prayer. Unrolling their rugs and facing Mecca, graceful as ballerinas, the Muslims began the routine: arms up (praise God and be thankful), arms on chest (forgive my sins), bowing (pray for others), down to the rug on knees (help me be humble), arms outstretched and forehead on the ground (thank God for listening), up then down; repeated several times and concluded with *Ameen* (Amen). The prayers finished; everyone climbed back into the train. Now we will continue to Khartoum.

The train didn't move.

"What's going on? Why are we stopped in the middle of the desert?" I asked my three companions in our first-class compartment.

"Trains don't usually stop at prayer time, do they? They didn't do so in Egypt," said Michael, an American physician.

"Well, I never heard of such a thing, but who knows. We're in a different country now," said Charles, a young man from England who was traveling with his sister, Mary.

"Why are you going to Khartoum?" asked Charles.

"I'm returning to Khartoum to rejoin my fiancé," I replied.

My fiancé! Thirty years old and that was the first time I uttered that phrase. I told them about my trip around the world and how love had changed my plan. I was going to get married in Sudan. Could it be real? Would we still like each other, love each other, after a two-week separation? Of course, I had doubts! Could I marry a European? Could I live in Sudan or wherever he may have a job? What was to be my life? Would I live in the USA ever again? Visit my family? Work professionally? Even work again?

"And why are you going to Khartoum?" I asked Charles and Mary. It was Mary's gap year, the year between high school and university. Charles had decided to take a year off from his studies to travel with his sister. They would visit several counties in Africa where their parents had been teachers as a young couple. Charles and Mary had flown from London to Cairo and were now headed south to Khartoum for a couple of weeks, then to Kenya and Tanzania, and complete their travels in India.

"Michael, why are you going to Khartoum?"

He responded he was without direction in his life and needed to get away. A medical doctor, he had spent two years in the army in Viet Nam. Returning home, broken by the horrors of war and the stress of military life, he and his wife had divorced. Living with his father wasn't working out. He decided to hit the road with a backpack and see where adventure took him.

A Sudanese family in the neighboring compartment informed us the locomotive had broken down, and the crew couldn't fix it. Another engine was on its way from Atbara and would hook up with our train in a few hours. A few extra hours. At least it was cool in the evening.

After decades of neglect, our first-class carriage was run down. I supposed our engine was too. However, the glory of better days was visible beneath the dust. Cracked leather seats on chipped hardwood benches, once exquisitely-gilded, wood paneling, and tarnished brass doorknobs and window fixtures revealed the elegance of yesteryear. This car could have been one of the first to arrive in Khartoum in the 1900s.

A military undertaking, the railway was built from Cairo to Khartoum by the British for use in General Horatio Kitchener's drive against the Mahdi in the late 1890s. Perhaps General Kitchener had ridden in this very car.

"Would you like some tea, Madam?" asked our porter dressed in the traditional flowing white robe and coiled-turban, bowing as he opened the door of our compartment. He served us hot, sweet tea, a staple of Sudanese hospitality, and afterward, brought us a typical meal of bread and boiled beans served in an aluminum bowl.

Clank, bang, neck-jarring clash—as expected, another engine arrived five hours later, and we started rolling down the track. We settled in for the night, preparing to sleep. We all wanted to stretch out, so the two men took the floor giving the bench seats to us two women. We expected the gentle swaying of the train to rock us like a baby's cradle; however, before we could fall asleep, the train slowed. Then stopped. It was close to midnight. We'd been traveling for only thirty minutes! We soon learned the second engine had broken down. Once again, we were stranded in the desert. And again, it was time for prayers. With water and rugs, people clamored out of the train to perform prayers in the moonlight. The solitude of the desert only enforced my feeling of being marooned. Fortunately, I wasn't alone.

Stars filled the sky, so close I thought I could touch them. Would we see falling stars? Would a spaceship rescue us tonight? Were there marauding bandits in the desert? Would they rob the foreigners first?

None of us slept much that night. The cockroaches thought it was New Year's Eve as they danced the night away—over us and everything in sight. Sleeping on the floor wasn't possible; the men got off the dance floor. Snuggling with our backpacks as support with legs and feet intertwined on the benches, we slept fitfully, surrounded by the fresh desert air coming through the open window. We awoke in the morning in the still-motionless train. The orange globe rising in the east promised another sweltering day.

Sunrise, time again for prayers. Our drinking water once again being used for bathing! Each train car had a traditional conical clay pot, called a *zehir*, filled with drinking water. Evaporation through the clay cooled the water inside. When full, the *zehir* held about ten gallons. Ours had less than three gallons remaining. How long would we be in the desert, how long would the water last?

Maybe I wouldn't get married. Perhaps we would never get to Khartoum. Was there enough food and water to see us through?

The porter arrived with breakfast, hot tea and a greasy fried-egg sandwich. It was ten o'clock in the morning; it was hot, already over 100°.

The relentless sun moved to the zenith. Again it was time for prayer. I hoped the people were praying for the arrival of the train engine. Again the porter brought us sweet, hot tea.

"Drink the hot tea, it's good for you," said Charles. "My parents told us to drink hot liquids during the hot, dry days in Sudan. The hot drink makes you sweat; so, you feel cooler."

Well, thinks this California gal from the Central Valley, I would rather have an iced drink. We clinked our glasses and drank up. And sweat we did, although I'm not sure I felt refreshed.

39

It was hot. It was dry. The scenery was tiresome. I was still reading *War and Peace*. However, I couldn't concentrate. Too hot. Out of boredom, we took a walk through the train cars to commiserate with our fellow sufferers.

Camel herders inhabited the entire third-class car at the end of the train. The old wagon must have been a cattle car at one time; benches had been bolted to the floor to create the illusion of a passenger coach. It looked like a gypsy camp, strewn with wooden camel saddles and brightly colored blankets, charcoal burners for making tea, loaves of bread, aluminum pots of cooked beans and baskets of peanuts. Being in the desert was routine for these guys. They had completed a six-week trek driving their camels to Egypt. Having sold them all, they were headed home to the western region of Sudan near El Fasher. It was comforting to know we had experienced desert men on our train.

Finally, clang, bang, neck-jarring clash—that could only mean one thing; another engine had arrived. We had sat immobile on the tracks for fourteen hours. This engine had traveled from Khartoum all night and morning to hook up to our stranded train. All aboard, we were finally going to move. Chugging along about 40 miles per hour, hour after hour, sand and more sand, we finally made it to Atbara, a town located on the Nile River.

Atbara has a rail yard, mostly a cemetery for dead engines. Possibly the two engines that gave out on our trip would have a funeral there. We were encouraged to visit the town while the engines were assessed and the train restocked. The homes and shops, constructed from Nile River mud bricks, blended with the colors of the sand. Everything was covered in fine dust, further obliterating the lines between buildings and the surroundings.

Just before sunset, we boarded the train, provisions replenished, our *zehir* full of water. One hundred eighty miles to Khartoum. I begged the universe: please let this engine be robust so we would have no more unscheduled stops in the desert. More beans and hot sweet tea for dinner. Another night with the cockroaches. Although sleep-deprived, we managed a few hours of deep sleep. The rhythmic music of the turning wheels, the gentle sway of the carriage through the sea of sand, on and on we traveled south. More hot sweet tea and fried egg sandwiches for breakfast. More monotonous scenery out the window.

We rejoiced when we saw buildings appear on the dusty horizon. We must be approaching Khartoum. It was mid-afternoon, the hottest part of the day, probably 110°. We slowly pulled into the train station. Loaded with boxes and bundles, chickens, and children, everyone began to disembark from the carriages and the roof of the train.

I saw Daniel from the window. He was pacing, marching, and probing the crowd for me. He spied me, raced towards me, helped me down from the carriage onto the concrete platform, and clasped me in his arms.

Trembling, and close to tears, he blurted, "What happened? I thought you had changed your mind. I stayed all day at the station yesterday. They told me the train had problems, but I thought you weren't coming back."

Finally, I'm off the train! Walking on solid ground.

"Two engines broke down. We sat for hours in the middle of the desert. Come, I want you to meet my new friends," I replied.

"I've been at the station since morning. I was ready to get in my plane and fly over the railroad tracks until I found you. Are you okay?" he questioned, not interested in meeting my friends.

"Let's get married tomorrow," he pleaded.

My fate is sealed. Khartoum will be my home.

Bicentennial

1976

The rumble of a distant cannon disturbed my sleep. The thunder of mortar shells penetrated my wakefulness. It was the Fourth of July 1976. My sleepy thoughts drifted back to childhood when this holiday started at daybreak with the boom of cannons from the park near our home, continuing hourly until sunset. On this day in 1976, patriotic celebrations were planned across the USA. Was Khartoum celebrating the United States Bicentennial?

Curious, I got out of bed; the sun had not yet pushed above the horizon. I wandered to the patio of our third-floor room in the Air Taxi rest house. From the terrace, we had an unobstructed view of the runway of the Khartoum International Airport.

To my surprise, hundreds of men were racing down the runway—white *jelabiyas* flapping like the sails of a boat, coiled turbans unfurling as they ran, flip-flops discarded when they broke. Why are they running away from the airport control tower?

"Daniel, come and look at this. Have you ever seen a Sudanese in such a hurry? What is all that noise?" I asked.

Sleepily, he joined me on the patio.

ZING—I ducked. I perceived something like a hummingbird whizzing by inches from my head. Then another. And another.

Daniel grabbed me by my T-shirt and yanked me into our room.

"Bullets! Those are bullets!" he shouted as he quickly slammed the door shut. He rushed downstairs to the telephone. He called the airport control tower. He was scheduled to fly that morning.

"Stay home, the airport is closed, we are under attack ..." then the phone went dead.

Daniel had been in the Belgian army and had been a soldier in the Belgian Congo. Danger excited him; perilous situations drew him in. I couldn't believe his first thought was to go to the airport to see what was happening. I was terrified. I wanted to find a bathtub—could a bullet penetrate a tub. I was sure any bullet shot my way would find me. I stayed away from the windows. I checked to make sure the doors were locked. Upstairs or downstairs, which would be the safest spot? Unfortunately, the rest house had no tubs.

"Don't go!" I begged. "This isn't your fight! I'm afraid. Don't leave me alone."

My pleading worked; he stayed with me. However, he anxiously paced the floor, eager for information. Do I really want to live in Khartoum? Is he the right man for me?

The three resident servants joined us in the living room. One of them turned on the TV, nothing. He tried the radio, only static. We had no idea what was happening.

After breakfast, Old Abdul—who we called Mr. Magoo because of his round face and failing eyesight—said there would be no more meals in the rest house until it was safe to go to the market.

Civil war between the north and the south wasn't new in Sudan. Following seventeen years of fighting, the country had been at peace for the past four years. Could the war have started again? Not knowing anything was unsettling. I had been bored before this day. Indeed, I wasn't bored on this Fourth of July. However, it wasn't the kind of excitement I craved. This was dangerous. This was my first time experiencing armed conflict. Little did I know it wouldn't be my last.

Sharia Matar (Airport Road), a major thoroughfare running parallel to the airport runway, was quiet; no cars, no taxis, no buses, and no people. It was eerie. An occasional shot rang out from the direction of the airport terminal.

At noon, we decided to cross the street to the German Club. Hearing an odd screeching sound, we stopped outside the compound gates when we saw two tanks crawling our way. This was no movie. I could have touched one as it caterpillared by us. Maybe this wasn't such a good idea.

When the coast was clear, we scampered across the road, hoping we would find lunch. Fortunately, the club had freezers, so there was food, perhaps a week's worth—unless the soldiers or militants discovered the provisions and showed up uninvited. The electricity went out as we ate lunch. How long would the food stay good?

By afternoon, I was no longer thinking about finding a protective bathtub. The streets were still abandoned; no traffic on Sharia Matar. We no longer heard mortars or gunshots. The next day was quiet too. However, we limited our travels to the German Club. We still didn't know what was going on.

On the third morning, the streets were quiet; a few cars ventured out on the main road. We hailed a taxi and headed to the Meridian Hotel where friends were staying. Walking from the parking lot, we heard gunshots ring out a block away. Daniel started to run towards the sound.

"Where the hell are you going?" I shouted at him as I ran in the opposite direction towards the hotel.

He turned, and when he saw the horror on my face, he joined me and we ran to the hotel. The Sudanese concierge swiftly opened the glass entry doors; we rushed in, and the doors were locked behind us. Quickly, we got away from all that glass. We took the elevator to our friend's room on the sixth floor where we watched the action play out below. Some men had on uniforms; some did not; they all had guns and were running, hiding, and shooting.

Please don't look up and see us here, I thought. Fortunately, no bullet found a home. No blood was shed in the melee as far as we could see.

As only a soldier would notice, Daniel remarked on the fact that the soldiers had no laces in their boots. How could they run? Could the battle be lost because of such a simple need? After thirty minutes, all was quiet. The rebels were either subdued or fled the scene. We had a nice lunch and a swim in the pool. The outside world seemed so far away.

In a few days, the city returned to normal. The markets and shops reopened. Cars, taxis, buses, and people flooded the streets. The army had won, had subdued insurgents from Libya. Three thousand combatants had been killed during the fighting. Soon afterward, a hundred rebels were executed.

I had survived. I felt stronger. I felt confident. I felt durable and resilient.

I expected to read about the fighting in the next *Newsweek* magazine. Nope. The bicentennial celebrations were a feature story. Operation Entebbe was on the cover—the Air France plane hijacked to Uganda. The successful hostage rescue of over one hundred passengers by the Israeli Army occurred on July Fourth. Sudan wasn't mentioned in the magazine. My family and friends in the USA wouldn't know I had been in danger that July Fourth, an eventful day I will never forget.

El Qasr Avenue

Sporting a cap with a glossy black visor, dressed in a khaki-colored uniform, epaulets boasting two stripes, black shoes shiny as mirrors, she stands on the three-foot-high concrete pedestal in the middle of the intersection of El Gamhuriya and El Qasr Avenues. Arms in constant, exaggerated motion ending in spotless white gloves, she conducts the steady flow of traffic. An occasional whistle shrieks out to an errant driver. Yes, women in Khartoum have professional, specialized, and skilled jobs.

With its shops, banks, and restaurants, El Gamhuriya was considered the main street of Khartoum. But for me, I traversed more miles, usually on foot, along El Qasr Avenue. Running from the train station on the southern end, then veering on both sides of the Palace (Qasr), the avenue ended at the Blue Nile River where huge, ancient trees—trees planted by the British before independence—spread their limbs to touch each other over the street.

CRSO

The wall around the Coliseum Cinema on El Qasr Avenue was constructed of bricks made in the traditional style of river mud, straw, and donkey manure. The concoction was hand mixed, then shaped in molds. After drying in the sun, the bricks were baked in the wood-fired kilns located on the banks of the Blue Nile River. Thick brown mud plaster covered the bricks of the wall, which was white-washed every decade or so. The next paint job was overdue. The wall, thick and tall, crumbled at the base.

Spikes, glass or barbed wire was not embedded on the top of this wall as was found on walls surrounding newer businesses. However, the wall was high enough that people could not look or jump over it. Viewing movies for free was not allowed at the Coliseum Cinema on El Qasr Avenue. The cinema was open only in the evening, only after dark as it had no roof. For a nickel, one could sit under the stars and enjoy a couple of hours of entertainment. The nickel ticket meant you sat on the ground. For a dollar, we sat in a private box seat with four white plastic chairs. As most chairs had cracked seats and splayed or broken legs, we carefully tested each chair before sitting.

Most movies were from India, Bollywood before that was a name. The plot was always the same—a beautiful young woman, a love-struck young man, song and dance to woo her, a problem or drama involving a weapon, resolution, and then more singing and dancing. Sometimes the movies were Egyptian; the same plot though not so much song and dance. However, a love-struck couple, a distraught mother, and a father or brother with a sword or knife appeared during the films. Subtitles covered half the screen—Arabic, English, and French. However, since most of the audience was illiterate, the subtitles were useless except for a few of us. Regardless of language, written or spoken, we all enjoyed the movies for their color, music, and theatrics. The dialogue didn't matter.

Living in the Air Taxi rest house, we had no amusements, no distractions. We were so bored that the silliness of the movies at the cinema was more fun than staring at the walls of our room. In later years, we had access to VHS and no longer visited the cinema.

However, I frequently walked past the cinema on El Qasr Avenue. The smell of the cinema wall never failed to assault my senses. Set back from the cracked sidewalk by twenty feet or so, the wall was a urinal for many men walking by. At any given time, as many as half a dozen men faced the wall. White robes hiked up to their waist, undergarments untied and discreetly lowered, the men would squat and relieve themselves against the base of the wall. The hot desert sun would bake the acidic liquid mixed with the crumbling mud to create a stench wafting up and down the street. I always walked on the opposite side of the sidewalk, held my breath, picked up my pace, and looked straight ahead.

I wonder if the wall is still standing.

⋈

I found a treasure on El Qasr Avenue: books, books, and more books. Classics, novels, history, thrillers, mysteries, romance, and biography: all in hardback, all in good condition, all in English! The U.S. Agency for International Development (USAID) funded the library. I immediately got a library card and checked out my allotment of books every week.

Before I got a job, living in the rest house was mind-numbing. Now, in addition to swimming and sitting around the pool at the German Club, I could read. I must have read half the books in that library. Thick books, thin books, interesting books, exciting books, boring books, I read them all. I packed a book along with me everywhere I went. In Khartoum, waiting is a given, in line for bread or gas, a medical appointment, and every government office. Book in hand, I could pleasantly pass the time by reading, a habit I continue to observe.

⋈

"What time is it?" someone behind me asked as we walked along El Qasr Avenue in front of the University of Khartoum, School of

Medicine. I turned to find a slim young man, his long legs quickly bringing him to my side.

"It's 9:30," I told him as I looked at my watch.

It was May, and already sweat was forming on my brow as the hot morning air promised another sweltering day.

"Welcome to my country; I hope you're enjoying your stay."

"Oh, I've been here for a few months. It sure is getting hot. Is it always like this?" I asked.

"Well, this is just the beginning. It will only get hotter. But have you tasted the wonderful watermelons we grow? Do you like mango? It's available all year round; in fact, you can pick them off the trees along the street. Just like the schoolboys do."

After extolling the virtues of life in Khartoum, the conversation ended with an invitation to have tea with his family. This same conversation, repeated many times over the years with strangers, always started with the same question *what time is it?* I soon learned that no one wanted to know the time. Appointments and needing to be somewhere at a particular time was a cultural rarity. It was just a pick-up line leading to a conversation, a gesture of friendship, and a show of national pride. Only rich people had wristwatches.

One time it was not in friendship. Automobile fuel was often in short supply. Hundreds of cars would line up at the gas station the day before one's weekly five-gallon ration ticket was valid.

Once while waiting in line, I heard someone mumbling at the back passenger door of my car.

"What did you say?" I turned to look and saw a young man backing further away toward my bumper.

"Huh, what did you say?" I asked again as I turned my body around to look at him.

"What time is it?" he asked.

I turned to look at my watch and saw my purse being snatched from the front passenger seat by another man. A purposeful distraction. Off they ran.

I usually kept the passenger door locked with the window rolled up. But I had given a friend a ride, and, when he got out of the car, I didn't lock the door or roll up the window. My purse was gone! My money was gone! My ration ticket was gone!

Bolting out of my car, shouting, "Stop, stop, thief, *harami*!" I ran after the young men. I caused quite a stir among the other people waiting for gas. Finally, the commotion alerted the station attendant who came to see me. I felt abused and tricked. My gas tank was almost empty. Fortunately, I was able to convince the attendant to let me have my five gallons of gas, and I promised to return with the money, which I did. To this day, I put my purse on the passenger seat but check to see that the window is up and the door locked.

Technology and oil revenues in Sudan have led to a higher standard of living and created a middle class. I understand most people now have cell phones and, therefore, know what time it is. I wonder what has replaced that phrase of introduction, "What time is it?"

The Pilot's Wife

1976–1977

"Don't ever marry a man until you have met his family," was the only marriage advice my mother gave me.

Daniel and I didn't get married the day after I returned from Egypt. Neither did we marry the next week nor the next month; I was in no rush. Did I need to meet his family first? In a country where a single woman isn't allowed alone with a man except her father or brother, where marriage was arranged between families and engaged couples were always attended by chaperones, I became the pilot's wife. We lived together. What else could I be?

No job, no household chores. Each day was a vacation—no schedules to decipher, no tickets to buy, no lodgings to procure; I had plenty of time to accompany Daniel on his flights with Khalil's Air Taxi. He enjoyed my company and showed me how to fly the plane; I sat in the right seat; thus, I became the co-pilot. With the stick between my legs, I kept the little airplane of the attitude indicator (the artificial horizon) straight on the centerline of the dial on the instrument panel. In plain English, that meant I kept the plane level and on the correct heading. It was hard work; the stick wasn't easy to maneuver. Holding that little plane in the exact position took all my attention. Even though I learned about wing design and lift, I am still amazed every time I see an airplane take off.

CRXSO

Daniel had two airline pilot licenses, American and Swiss. However, he preferred the smaller bush planes he flew by looking out the window. Flying for Air Taxi was a step up from the agricultural flying he had done in several African countries. Sudan was flat, roads and railroads, the usual landmarks, were few and far between. The desert heat produced severe updrafts, causing a small plane to bump and bounce in the air. When dust limited visibility, he flew with instrument navigation (IFR). Thankfully, there were few other aircraft to contend with. He felt safer in the air than on the ground. And soon, I felt more comfortable in a small plane than in a jumbo jet.

One of the first trips I took with Daniel taught me a science lesson—gases expand as the plane increases altitude and air pressure decreases.

"Was that your stomach?" I asked Daniel.

"No, I thought that was you."

Then again, gurgles and belches. We were the only two people in the plane. Then we heard it again, louder.

"Are you sure that wasn't you?"

"No, not me. I think the sound is coming from behind us. It must be him!"

A wooden casket lay behind our seats in the cargo hold. We were delivering a rich old man, very dead, to his home village for burial. It was creepy, then smelly. Physics, biology, atmospheric conditions—so much to learn in a most unlikely place.

One time a wealthy live man rented Air Taxi to take him to his ancestral home for a religious ceremony. We landed near his village in the morning and expected him back in three hours. We waited on the dirt runway. No airport, no facilities, no food, no chairs, we leaned against the wheels of the plane in the shade under the wing. I'm sure glad we had brought water and snacks. The afternoon sun was low in

In the shade of the Pilatus Porter

the sky; we were still waiting. We needed to be back in Khartoum before nightfall. As the sun was setting, we left the village without him. A few days later, we found out the man objected to the presence of a woman in the plane when he was going to partake in a religious gathering. I felt guilty. We were not yet sensitive to the role of women in this Muslim country. After that, Daniel asked his passengers' permission for me to come along.

There are no toilets in small planes. However, the pilot has a piss tube. Just like it sounds, a funnel atop a plastic tube that drains outside the airplane. Moisture in the air—are you sure it's rain? There is a skill to using one of these as the suction release valve can suck down more than piss. For me, I planned my liquid consumption carefully and always took advantage of the available facilities, sometimes a bush, before boarding the plane.

As the afternoon heat increased, the plane could be tossed around by rising currents. Daniel loves to tell stories of people getting airsick—filling seasick bags, thermoses, lunch pails, and one time a Stetson Hat.

Daniel flew a bright red-orange Pilatus Porter, a STOL aircraft capable of Short Take-Offs and Landings. This plane, designed in Switzerland, could take off and land on the short runways in the Alps. A Mack Truck of an airplane, it was perfect in Sudan on the rough, dirt runways, sometimes only a track cleared of brush.

A Pilatus Porter skeleton lay next to the runway in the town of Malakal. A couple of years before I arrived, a British pilot tried to impress the Sudan Airlines staff with the STOL capabilities of the plane by taking off across the runway. He didn't make it. Fortunately, everyone aboard walked away unhurt. However, it's disturbing to land there in the Pilatus Porter next to the skeleton of a sister plane.

A storm in Malakal in the south of Sudan claimed the life of our friend Captain Sukkar, the co-pilot who flew with Daniel the first time we met. With a tropical thunderstorm approaching, Sukkar departed for Khartoum. He headed downwind to take off, the wrong way, and never got enough lift to get airborne. Unfortunately, no one survived the crash.

During the next couple of years, three more pilots we knew from the rest house would die in aviation accidents; Jean-Claude on an oil rig; Gunter and Michel in a Lear Jet. Gunter, Daniel's former chief pilot, had taken a job in Athens and asked Daniel to be his co-pilot. Daniel was not a right-seat pilot (co-pilot); he declined, undoubtedly saving his life.

CRSO

Every evening we had dinner on the freshly cut lawn at the German Club. As restaurants were scarce in Khartoum, the club became a gathering place of ex-pats. Gunter and Renee, Frantz and Helen, Daniel and I, and other pilots staying in the Air Taxi rest house, would meet for drinks and dinner and conversation. Renee spoke only French, I spoke only English, Daniel spoke French and English, Frantz spoke German and English, and Helen and Gunter spoke all three languages. Dinner with polyglots sounded like the Tower of Babel. Indeed, I missed two-thirds of the conversation, and yet, the gin and lemonade helped make the evening ring with laughter and wellbeing.

We told tales of our homeland, of our families, of our travels, and, most important, what was available or not in the markets.

The Sudanese waiters, dressed smartly in their long white *jelabiyas* and rolled white turbans, spoke English. At least they knew the words of the food and drink that were available—Wienerschnitzel, Nile perch, beefsteak, french fries, and gin, whiskey, and beer.

CRSO

"I need to get a job!" I exclaimed, literally bored to tears. The vacation was over. "If I am going to stay in Khartoum, I need to do more than fly with you once in a while! And I'm ready to get married."

After six months with Daniel, I felt my future was uncertain. I was bored. I was thirty years old. I wanted children. My biological clock was ticking. However, I wanted a husband first. I hadn't met Daniel's family. I was ready to disregard my mother's advice. However, Daniel was no longer prepared to tie the knot. He was thirty-six years old; he had managed without a wife so far. He didn't care one way or the other if he had kids. Why get married?

CRSO

The taxi rattled along El Qasr Avenue downtown then pulled into the small parking lot of the Stack Labs belonging to the Ministry of Health. Six stories tall, modern architecture, the building was sandwiched between the central government hospital and the

55

University's School of Medicine. I had second thoughts about going to my job interview when I saw bullet holes from sprays of machine-gun fire on the wall facing the parking lot.

The pathologist in the hematology lab, Dr. Anwar, handsome, jovial, and plump, greeted me with warmth. After a brief conversation, he offered me a job. He had several special projects he wanted to do and thought I could

Stack Lab Building

implement them. The work hours were 7 a.m. to 2 p.m. six days a week with Friday off. I later learned all the staff arrived at about 8 a.m. and left at 1 p.m. if the work was finished. Assuming I was a Christian, I could have Sundays off if I wanted to go to church. I would earn $200 a month, substantially less than I could make at home, but almost double what the Sudanese technicians earned. However, it wasn't about the money; it was about keeping my mind active and working professionally.

On my first day at work, I met the staff. Gadura, the chief technician, aloof and arrogant, over six feet tall, towered over the rest of us. Awad, his assistant, was cock-sure and had a chip on his shoulder. I think they felt threatened by my American education and professional background. Sharif did most of the work. He didn't have a diploma as the others did; nonetheless, he had been trained by the professional staff. Asma, wrapped in her multicolored *toub* from head to ankles, was all smiles and was prone to giggles. She became my friend and several times invited me to her home to have a meal with her family. Amal was beautiful and sophisticated, exquisitely coiffed though she covered her hair with her *toub*. Flawless make-up, she looked like a model. She would soon depart for six months of maternity leave.

I wondered how women could work wearing their national costume. About nine yards long, a *toub* is tucked under one arm and then wrapped about the body a couple of times and then over the head. Worn over a dress, the colorful wraps are an essential part of a woman's wardrobe. Asma and Amal were able to perform their work flawlessly despite needing to adjust the *toub* from time to time.

After a few weeks, Gadura and Awad invited me to join the group for the ten o'clock breakfast. The traditional meal of beans, raw onions, and white cheese was scooped up with torn bits of flatbread. I think they finally realized I wouldn't upset the balance in the lab.

The hematology lab received about a hundred blood samples every day from the hospital. Sharif prepared the blood smears and the samples for analysis. As soon as the blood smears dried, he placed the slides in stacks because flies would eat the blood right off the glass. The technical staff, including me, performed the analysis. I relearned manual techniques that hadn't been used in American clinical labs for twenty years.

The lab, on the ground floor, was dark. The small windows, located high along one wall, were always open to allow fresh air and flies into the room. Only half the light fixtures worked. The wooden workbenches were scarred and stained from decades of use. Broken chairs were stacked in the corner of the room.

Nevertheless, the staff performed the tests as best as they could. I was thrilled to be working. Never mind the bullet holes in the wall.

Moving Day

"Oh, please, madam. I'm honest. I work hard. I live in the building so I can help you do anything at any time. I'll do your shopping, cooking, washing, ironing, anything you want," said Hilou, a thin young man recently displaced from his home in Eritrea.

After seven months of living in one room in the rest house, Daniel and I moved to a furnished apartment across the river in Khartoum North. By that time, we had our own set of wheels—a 100cc maroon motorcycle. Motorcycles were rarely seen in Khartoum; Daniel was probably the only *kwawaaja* to have one. We must have been a sight on moving day. Clutching Daniel's suitcase, I balanced on the back as he maneuvered through traffic across the Blue Nile Bridge. Our apartment was on the eighth floor of the tallest building on the north side of the river.

"But don't worry," said Osman, the Air Taxi clerk who waited with the keys outside the building, "There's an elevator."

He didn't tell us the elevator started on the second floor and went as high as the seventh floor. We soon found out that it was often broken.

We were excited to have our own place. I could cook our meals. We would entertain friends. We would have a private bathroom. No longer would I need to get dressed to go to the toilet at night.

My backpack loaded on my back, apartment keys in my pocket, we made our second trip across the Blue Nile. In one hand, I cradled a small clay pot with a plant and clung on to Daniel with the other. The purple, red, yellow, and green miniature peppers of the Bolivian rainbow pepper plant bounced as we hit the potholes in the bumpy roads. I have been a gardener all my life. To make the rest house more personal, I had bought this little plant and now brought my garden to our new home.

The apartment seemed enormous. With only the contents of one suitcase and one backpack, we settled into our new home in twenty minutes. The pepper plant sat on the dining table; home is where the garden is.

Looking back, I realize the apartment was tiny; one bedroom with a bed and a dresser. The main room had four functional chairs surrounding a coffee table and a dining table with two chairs. Entertaining may be difficult. How many of our friends would climb eight stories to spend an evening with us, anyway?

The kitchen had a gas cooker with two burners, the butane tank next to it took up a quarter of the floor space. The refrigerator was no taller than a child; I had to bend down to get anything out of it. Two cooking pots, four plates, four cups, four forks, four of all the necessary eating implements. My camping kitchens were bigger and better equipped than this one. Be creative, rise to the challenge. At least I have a kitchen and can cook what we want.

The bathroom contained the essentials—a western toilet, a small sink, and a showerhead over a porcelain basin. No shower curtain meant the floor would often be wet. No hot water doomed us to cold showers during the winter. In the summer, we wanted a refreshing shower; but the water was scalding from the sun radiating on the water pipes. Although it was a small step up from the rest house, it was a step in the right direction. We had privacy. We had shelter. We had a sanctuary. We had a view of the Nile from our front door.

The next day, Hilou was there again, begging to be our house servant. Why would I need or even want a servant? I thought domestic help was comparable to slavery.

The rest house staff had done everything—shopping, cooking, cleaning, and washing clothes. I had been bored living in one room; I missed doing household chores. A small apartment? I would show Daniel my domestic skills and be happy to do so.

That lasted one week, waiting in line to buy our bread every day, removing the ever-present dust from the furniture and floor daily, washing clothes on my hands and knees in the shower basin. I tracked down Hilou and became his employer.

CRSO

During one of Daniel's overnight trips to Juba, rebel fighters attacked the town and airport. Bullet holes pierced Daniel's plane, the Pilatus Porter, parked on the tarmac. An American pilot panicked, and as he took off for Nairobi, the aircraft was shot down and he died. Fortunately, Daniel didn't feel the need to investigate; he stayed put in his rest house. The airport closed for several days as fighting continued around the town.

Daniel had no news from Khartoum and imagined me home alone and in danger. Was there fighting in Khartoum? Concerned for my safety, he realized how much he loved me.

One week later, when the airport reopened, Frantz, the Air Taxi aircraft engineer, went to Juba to repair the plane. After a test flight, Daniel and Frantz safely returned to Khartoum.

The next day, crossing the bridge over the Blue Nile on our motorcycle, Daniel turned back to me and shouted, "Let's get married."

"When?" I shouted back.

"Tomorrow!" he replied.

Finally, we both agreed to marry. The next day we went to the civil service government agency to find out how we could get married.

"Fill out this form and bring it here tomorrow. And bring some flour," stated Bahig Sourial, the Registrar of Marriage. Flour? Maybe he meant flowers? I was puzzled. What would flour have to do with a wedding?

Daniel asked his chief pilot, Gunter, to be his witness. I asked Rosie, a work colleague from Scotland, to stand with me.

"We have to get our hair done. What should I wear? Do you have a nice dress?" squealed Rosie.

I think she was more excited than me. Since most people thought we were already married, I didn't want to make a big deal out of the official ceremony.

My Sudanese work colleagues couldn't believe I asked for only one day off to get married. Sudanese couples take several weeks of vacation when they get married. However, I declined the offer; I didn't need weeks to prepare for our wedding. What would I do anyway? Work at the lab was the most fulfilling hours of my day.

On March 10, 1977, appropriately coiffed, fingernails painted, I put on my best dress. Daniel wore long pants, unusual for him. We met Gunter and Rosie downtown, and the four of us, with flour and flowers in hand, went to the registrar's office. Each with a hand on a Bible, we recited the Non-Mohammedan Marriage vows. Then we each repeated, "I do."

The registrar instructed us to "sign your names or make your marks."

We all signed the official documents. We were married. The ceremony was over in less than five minutes. I never did find out about the flour or flowers. Furthermore, I had not followed my mother's advice.

We had lunch at the restaurant in the newly-opened Hilton Hotel. After lunch, Gunter invited us to his house to celebrate with champagne. Thirty-one-years-old. I was a bride.

We went home to our little apartment. I thought nothing had changed; we just signed some papers. However, I felt different. I felt secure. I felt loved. We would plan our future together. I stopped taking my birth control pills. Our lives began to improve exponentially.

Champagne toast on our wedding day

Street Thirty-Seven

1977–1982

With a shaky hand, Ahmed scrawled an X on the paper he could not read. His fingers clutched the pen as if it would slip away. We asked him to stay on as our house servant in our new home and needed him to sign a contract of employment.

Daniel had a new job. After flying with Daniel on many Air Taxi flights, the Belgian manager of a construction company decided to buy an airplane. The company had a contract with the Sudanese Government to build the Melut Sugar Refinery in the south of Sudan. Daniel researched the best plane for the job and was rewarded with the position as the pilot. His salary tripled, our benefits surpassed all expectations—a house, car, servants, insurance—the usual perks of an ex-pat employee.

Relocating from Khartoum North across the river to Street Thirty Seven in the New Extension of Khartoum meant we were moving up in the world. We would be neighbors with embassies and ambassadors, diplomats, churches, mosques, and the best-stocked grocery store in town. We loaded our meager possessions, including my pepper plant, into the car we were given and made one trip across the Blue Nile to our new home. We left behind the eight flights of stairs and honeymoon memories.

Along with Ahmed, we inherited the contents of the upstairs duplex from a German couple leaving Khartoum. The furniture—

chairs, bookshelves, bed frame, and tables—had been built from packing crates sent from Germany when they had arrived several years earlier. The cushions for the chairs were made from good German material and stuffed with Sudanese cotton. The mattress was constructed in the traditional style— local cotton fabric stuffed with cotton batting grown in the fields near Khartoum.

Our new home - upstairs

Also included were dishes, pots and pans, sheets, tablecloths, as well as supplies unavailable in Khartoum like good quality light bulbs. We were delighted with our new home. Our status in the community improved.

The new plane was an executive model Piper Navajo. Mr. Frere, the project manager, flew in luxury. However, when the leather seats were removed, it became a cargo plane. Daniel loved his new job and the brand new aircraft he had flown from Belgium.

CR£O

View of our neighborhood

Several months later, while preparing breakfast, I felt a surprising tingle in my belly. Could I be pregnant? I wanted to be pregnant. Children were not a priority in Daniel's life, but I wanted children. I wanted to experience pregnancy, a new life within me. I felt I would have missed a vital aspect of womanhood if it were not to be. Knowing how important it was to me, we had decided to have children when we got married almost a year ago. Daniel was an only child and admitted he was spoiled.

"One is not good. Look at me! But when my parents saw what they got, they didn't dare have another!" he exclaimed. "If we're going to have one, I think we should have at least one more."

I was in my early thirties, afraid I had waited too long. A few weeks later, a lab test confirmed what I'd suspected.

I was elated. Daniel was delighted. Now that a child was on the way, at thirty-eight-years-old, he eagerly looked forward to becoming a father. I began to collect baby things from the departing international community. People leaving Sudan sell or give away personal belongings as merchandise in the shops was limited. I converted one of our three bedrooms into a nursery.

Helen, my Swiss friend, had given birth to her two daughters in Khartoum without any problems. I wanted to have our baby in Khartoum too. I believe childbirth to be a natural phenomenon, not a medical problem. I would see an OB/GYN doctor during our annual leave in California, and if all looked normal, I would give birth in Khartoum. I wanted Daniel to be there, wanted to go home as a family after the birth.

The pregnancy progressed smoothly. I loved showing off my growing belly. I got out my sewing machine and made maternity dresses. I would be a mother. I will never forget the first time I felt the baby move. Nothing compares to that feeling, a body different than mine kicking me, growing inside me. New life! A girl? A boy? Maybe both? It didn't matter. Who would that person become? A condition as old as life itself, and yet, to me, it was a triumph, a longing fulfilled. A miracle. A mystery. A new soul.

Other than fatigue, I felt terrific; my skin glowed, my breasts grew. No longer was I taking care of just myself. Everything I ate, every emotion I felt, every thought I had was shared with this baby inside me. I continued working at the hospital lab. I walked the neighborhood every morning and swam at the American Club every afternoon.

That summer, when I was six months pregnant, Daniel and I went to Belgium and then California for our annual leave. His parents were overjoyed to become grandparents for the first time. They were in their seventies and had given up hope of ever becoming grandparents. My parents were delighted to welcome their fourth grandchild. How fun it was to shop for baby things in California.

Due to my age of thirty-three years, my doctor in California performed an ultrasound. Not only did he tell me the pregnancy looked normal but announced that we were having a boy. I was relieved when he said there was no reason I should not deliver our son in Khartoum.

Jean-Marc Xavier was born in September 1978. Chubby and bald, ten fingers and ten toes. He was perfect. He was a delight. He rarely cried. He gurgled and laughed, and I did too. He was swimming before he crawled. His baldness gave way to thick golden hair. His long dark eyelashes were going to drive the little girls wild. He was good-natured, coordinated, cheerful, and stubborn. Had my conscious thoughts of happiness and joy reached him during the pregnancy? Little did I know he would be with us for just a few short years.

Soba Hospital and my work colleagues

Intending to go back to work after Xavier was born, I interviewed several young women to be his nanny. Finding something deficient in all candidates—didn't speak English, lacking personal hygiene, no experience with babies—I decided to be a stay-at-home mom.

"But you have to go back to work!" demanded Daniel. "If you don't work, you can't live in my house!"

I couldn't believe it! I was furious! How could I leave my precious two-month-old son with a stranger I couldn't even talk with? My job had relocated to Soba Hospital fifteen miles away from town in the middle of nowhere. I didn't have a car. The car and house belonged to Daniel's company. I used transportation provided by the hospital to get to and from work. Telephones were not available. What if something went wrong? What if Xavier became sick or fell out of bed, or the nanny left?

My initial desire to work in Sudan had been to occupy my time. Now I wanted to be a full-time mother. Daniel absolutely refused. He said if I stayed home, I would get fat, lazy, and dull. One of the reasons he married me, he said, was because I did not need to rely on him. I was not a dependent wife, as most the other ex-pat women were. I was not only facilitating Daniel's life; I could take care of myself. That gave him comfort in case he could not do so.

It was an ultimatum! We shouted. We argued. I cried. I considered leaving Daniel, leaving Sudan. I was close to ending my marriage. Either I work, or I don't live in his house! Thirty-three years old, blessed with a beautiful son, I wanted us to be a family, for Xavier to grow up knowing his father. I gave in and went back to work.

CREKO

All too soon, there was trouble with the sugar project. The Sudanese Government was not completing its part of the contract. The Belgian company was not getting paid for its work. The project was in jeopardy. After nearly two years, the project came to an end. The sugar factory was never built.

Again, our lives would only get better. Daniel was offered the best job of his career. And I, too, would have my dream job.

The United Nations (UN) had many missions in Sudan. However, air travel within Sudan was limited and unreliable. It was both expensive and inconvenient for UN staff to manage their projects efficiently outside Khartoum. Therefore, the United Nations International Children's Fund (UNICEF) decided to buy an airplane.

Once more, Daniel was asked to research which plane would be appropriate for the job. And once again, he was awarded the position as the pilot. No other pilots were working for the UN, so there was no pay scale assigned to the profession. When asked what salary he anticipated, he started at an extraordinary level, expecting to negotiate. When asked to justify such a high pay scale in the organization, he replied: "If you pay peanuts, you get monkeys." He got the job on the professional level he requested.

In January 1980, Daniel left for New York City for orientation and to sign his contract of employment with UNICEF. After completing the paperwork at headquarters, he went to Toronto, Canada, to pick up the plane, a twin-engine, 18-passenger, de Havilland Twin Otter. Three months later, when his training was complete, he flew the plane from Toronto to Khartoum, without an autopilot, without radar, and without GPS navigation. Flying only during the daytime, the trip of 7700 miles took seven days.

UNICEF Twin Otter

When it came to the airplane, Daniel was in charge. For safety, he insisted on taking off at 6 a.m., daybreak, before the heat of the day created challenging updrafts bouncing the plane in every direction. His boss, Chief of Mission for UNICEF, was not a morning person. He told Daniel they would depart at 8 a.m. when he visited the mission sites outside of Khartoum.

Daniel said, "No, we depart at 6 a.m."

"I'm your boss, and I decide when we leave," his boss replied.

Daniel said, "When you are aboard this plane, I'm the boss! We leave at 6 a.m. for your safety!" They always left at 6 a.m.

Daniel's Mediterranean temperament—his mother was from the south of France—kicked in when passengers weren't ready before 6 a.m. He would stomp around the plane, kick the tires, and swear in French—traits he exhibited when I met him so many years earlier. I heard it said that some people who didn't know him were afraid to fly with such an agitated pilot. But once in the cockpit, he was focused and dedicated, and he always arrived safely.

After I returned to live in California, I met a man who asked me, after hearing my last name: "Do you know a pilot in Sudan?" Anyone who flew with him remembered him, one way or another. Ask Mother Teresa, Bob Geldorf, Ted Kennedy, Liv Ulman, Audrey Hepburn; I bet they remember flying with him. Darn—he retired too early to fly Angelina!

He was adventurous, courageous, and fearless (except when departing at 8 a.m.). Danger thrilled him. During rebel fighting in the south of Sudan, he flew into a remote village, landed on an abandoned airstrip, and rescued five young English citizens working for the British equivalent of the Peace Corps. For this, he received a letter of recognition from Margaret Thatcher, the British Prime Minister.

CR☙

In 1980, I was at work at Soba Hospital when an American man came to visit the lab. Professor Bennet was in Khartoum for one year to set up a tropical disease research lab. Another professor at Michigan State University (MSU) had procured a multimillion-dollar grant from the National Institutes of Health (NIH) to study four significant diseases in Sudan—malaria, schistosomiasis, leishmaniasis, and onchocerciasis. The outcome of meeting Professor Bennet resulted in a job offer to provide technical expertise to the project. I had no idea that the meeting would become a turning point in my professional career.

Me in my office at MSU Lab

The tropical disease research lab was located downtown in the Stack Labs, where I had first started working. Major renovations were needed to support a modern, sophisticated research lab. The rooms were gutted. New floors, new ceiling, modern lighting, new benches, and cupboards were installed. The electrical wiring was upgraded for modern heavy-duty research equipment—a Scintillation counter, two ultra-low freezers, negative air-flow hood, and other sophisticated equipment. I set up two distilleries as the project would need triple distilled water for the high-quality analysis. Before that time, my work had been routine, doing the same tasks every day. Now I would have a chance to shine, to learn new skills. I dedicated myself to the success of the project.

When the lab was fully functional, graduate students from the University of Khartoum Medical School performed the analysis of the blood samples from patients with the diseases being studied.

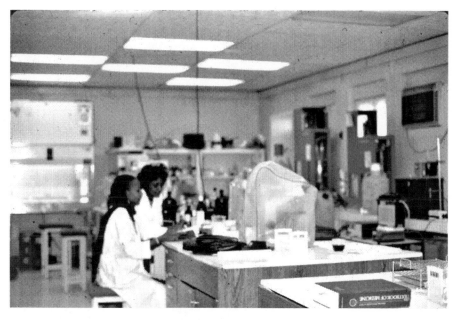

Students working at MSU Lab

My job changed to administrative work. I found I was good at organization and project management. I learned how to run the massive 50 kVA diesel generator we had for backup electricity. I procured the fuel for both the project vehicles and the generator. My duties also included supply management, rest house liaison, local payroll and finances, and contact between several American and Sudanese Government agencies. Professors from MSU brought teams of medical students from Michigan to do fieldwork. I organized all aspects of the visits—airport pickups at all hours of the day and night, securing travel permits, and obtaining project supplies. I also readied the rest house with food and sundry items for the visiting researchers. From the research, dozens of scientific papers were published in respected journals. Our project became known in the international medical research community. Researchers from seven different countries became involved in the project. The lab was a showcase for what could be accomplished under challenging conditions.

CRSO

We moved in diplomatic circles. We attended receptions for visiting dignitaries. During an official visit from New York, the executive director of UNICEF visited our home for afternoon tea.

I recall one evening at an official reception when a career diplomat spoke to me about his work. I talked about my work. He asked me questions and was impressed with my knowledge. All of a sudden, I realized I was on equal footing with him, with a diplomat. Not only did I fit in, but I also belonged to this community.

I felt sophisticated, adventurous, and knowledgeable. New arrivals to Khartoum were sent my way. I knew where to buy the freshest eggs, to find flour without weevils, and to hire the best plumber. I was appreciated. I was respected. I was valued. I realized I had a contribution to make—to my family, to my friends, to society.

No longer was I a backpacker. Now we traveled in business class.

Life was good. We both had exciting jobs; we lived in a lovely place; our son was healthy and growing. Only one thing was missing, another child.

Not My Enemy

1978

I delivered the handwritten invitation. The appropriate forms were filled out. A copy of our passports and a letter from UNICEF stating our character and employment were provided as requested. Their embassy approved the visit. The Russians were coming to our house for afternoon tea.

The Cold War with Russia was in its third decade. In grammar school, I had practiced hiding under my desk in case Russia launched a nuclear attack. My neighbors had built a bomb shelter in their backyard. Bob Dylan sang, "I've learned to hate Russians all through my whole life." Jimmy Carter boycotted the Olympic Games held in Moscow. Nevertheless, I had invited the enemy for tea.

A few years earlier, the Russians built Soba Hospital fifteen miles south of Khartoum. Russian doctors staffed the hospital and trained the Sudanese doctors and medical students.

The Ministry of Health Laboratories in the Stack Building where I worked moved to Soba Hospital. The hospital was so far from town that transportation to the new lab was provided for all employees. I lived two blocks from where the Russian doctors lived; consequently, I was told I could ride to the hospital with them.

I had never met any Russians. Aren't they the enemy? I was apprehensive as I walked to their building for the first time. Did they know I was to ride with them? Did they know I was an American—the only American working at Soba Hospital? Had the Russians learned to hate Americans?

The van arrived; I took a seat in the front row. Soon four men and one woman left the apartment building and approached the van. They nodded to me as they boarded, the woman sat in the seat behind me.

Looking straight ahead, uncomfortable and uncertain, I sensed someone leaning toward me. "Good morning, my name is Maye."

Maybe they aren't all Russians, I thought. She has no accent. I turned to see a beautiful Asian woman with long, straight, dark hair; clear, bronze skin; a lovely smile, and sparkling eyes. She appeared to be a few years older than me.

"Hi. My name's Sheila. You speak English so well."

"Oh," she laughed. "I have a degree in English Literature; I graduated from UCLA. I'm the interpreter for the doctors; none of them speak English, not even my husband."

She and her husband were from Kazakhstan, at that time a state in the Union of Soviet Socialist Republics (USSR). The others were from Moscow. They were in Khartoum for five years to establish the hospital radiology department.

At first, the doctors seemed distant and unfriendly; maybe they were only shy. The usual morning greeting was a slight nod as they entered the van. Of course, not having a common language was a barrier. Did they fear me? The American? During our drive to the hospital, Maye always sat on the seat behind me. We'd chat on our way to work. We talked about our families, our education, the weather, our lives in our home country—safe topics for citizens of warring nations.

The wives of the three other doctors had accompanied their husbands to Khartoum. However, their children stayed home in Russia. Maye told me it was assurance the parents would go back home when their contract was finished.

They weren't allowed to go out in public alone. All Russian citizens in Sudan traveled in groups of two or three wherever they went. They could socialize only with other Russians and could not attend public events without permission from their embassy. And yet, Maye and I were comfortable talking with each other. She was not my enemy. All of us were in Khartoum to share our professional knowledge.

The day of the tea arrived. Maye, the doctors, and their wives were driven to our home by a driver from their embassy.

Upon entering, I heard exclamations of joy, shrieks of laughter, and rapid conversation among the women.

"What are they saying?" I asked Maye. I was puzzled by their reaction.

"They say your house is like a museum. You have books, VHS movies, and music tapes. Can they look at your family photos? Where did you get this?" she asked, pointing to a batik of an African woman.

"Sure, make yourselves at home," I said, confused by their enthusiasm.

We had personal items in our home—wall hangings, baskets, copperware, candles, house plants. To me, it was nothing special; the decorations were inexpensive items found in the shops around Khartoum. Through Maye, we talked about our families, our work at the hospital, the usual exchange among friends. We had tea and sandwiches in the living room. All in all, it was a pleasant afternoon. The women thanked me profusely as they left, shaking my hand, and making eye contact. We weren't enemies.

Several months later, the Russian wives invited me to their apartments. I didn't need permission from my embassy. Probably they needed permission to ask me.

The Sudanese Ministry of Health furnished their apartments. I am sure the apartment looked the same as it had on the day they moved in five years earlier. No pictures on the wall, no books. Each couple had four plates, four cups, four forks, and four knives, enough for one couple to live modestly. It reminded me of our little apartment, our first home in Khartoum North, where I brought my pepper plant, making a house our home.

Each couple brought chairs and tea service from their apartment to where we all gathered, nine of us squeezing into one sitting room. Now I knew why they were so captivated by my home. We drank tea; we were relaxed. We were having a good time sharing stories. We were ambassadors of goodwill.

I had learned to hate the Russians. The Cold War had made me fear these people. However, hate and fear had no place in our acquaintanceship. Pearl S. Buck writes in *The Good Earth* "during a war... don't forget the humanity and culture of the decent people." John Lennon asked me to "Imagine all the people living life in peace..." We were decent people; we saw the good in each other. I can imagine, "all the world will be as one..."

Rocks and Onions

1982

"**D**own, Down, USA!" shouted the demonstrators marching down the main street of Khartoum. Placards scrawled in Arabic punctured the sky. The message—shouted in English—was loud and clear: *I need to get out of here*! I was running errands for work and quickly realized the chores were no longer critical. Like all the drivers ahead of me, I quickly turned my car around intending to return to my office.

For decades, the United States was a primary provider of military and economic aid to the Sudanese Government. At the time of the demonstrations, the Sudanese president, Jaafar Nimeiry, was in the United States receiving medical treatment. In an attempt to control the recent devaluation of the Sudanese pound, the United States and the International Monetary Fund (IMF) mandated the Sudanese Government to stop subsidizing food, fuel, and other commodities. The cost of gasoline suddenly went up 30 percent, and the price of sugar rose 60 percent. Sugar was a staple in both hot and cold drinks in every Sudanese home. The people—men and women—took to the streets in what is now called the Sugar Riots.

I tried to drive back to my office, but more protesters blocked the way. I kept driving following the cars ahead of me, not sure where I was going. When I saw another group of demonstrators who would soon meet police dressed in full riot gear, I pulled into a narrow alley, jumped out of the car and ran. I saw a man waving his arms, guiding me and a few others through a small doorway. We crouched as we rushed inside; the metal door clanged shut and was quickly bolted, locking us inside the small storage shed. I figured we were probably close to the central market. With a heavy sigh, I sat down on a stack of bags. Looking around, I realized not only was I the only foreigner, but I was also the only woman. A dozen men dressed in *jelabiya* and turbans had also taken refuge with me. There was little conversation or eye contact among us. We sat quietly amid the stacks of white woven plastic sacks containing flour, sugar, and rice. Then tear gas began seeping through the cracks of the shed.

No one knew where I was. I felt so alone, powerless, and bewildered. I wasn't sure what was going on, but certainly, I wouldn't discuss my nationality. Was this crowd after me? An American? Sudan had been my home—my home for seven years. I had nothing to do with government policies.

Chaos ensued outside the warehouse. I heard shouts and screams as rocks and clubs hit their targets. Through a tiny crack in the door, we saw the police—protected by shields and helmets—beat the demonstrators with batons and whips.

I was surprised hundreds of people were protesting—especially the number of women. Previous rebellions I had witnessed had been between military factions, not against the populace. The Sudanese people are kind and gentle. This activity was so out of character.

I wanted to go home. How long would I be here? What about my car abandoned in the alleyway? Xavier was at the French school far from the center of town. Daniel was in his office a few miles away. Were they safe? No one knew where I was! No one knew I was in trouble!

About an hour later, the area was quiet; the tear gas had dispersed. The owner of the shed slowly opened the door and peered outside.

Only a few police remained on the street. We left our sanctuary, thanking the owner as we ducked out the door into the alley.

My car was still where I had left it! The doors were still locked; the front and back windows were gone. The seats were covered in shattered glass; in addition to the glass, I was surprised to see not only rocks but onions too. What unlikely weapons! I was afraid to drive the vehicle, to drive in the streets. It was a mess, and I wasn't even sure it would start. What if someone hijacked it from me?

My office was about a mile away; I thought it would be safer to walk there. When I got to the building, my colleagues cheered. They knew I had gone downtown and were concerned for my safety. We climbed the stairs to the roof of the six-story building to survey the town. A few demonstrators near the train station a block away still held up their banners. Otherwise, the city looked quiet.

There had been disturbances in town the past couple of weeks. Hence, UNICEF had given me a walkie-talkie which I had left in my office. I radioed the UNICEF office to tell Daniel to come and get me at work.

He was there in a heartbeat. "Love-Love, what happened? Are you okay? Where is the car? We need to get the car!" he demanded.

"NO! We can't go back to the central market! I don't want to drive the car. I want to go home. Where is Xavier? We need to get him from school. What's going on in our neighborhood? I want to go home."

By now, it was early afternoon. We rode home on Daniel's motorcycle through the quiet streets. I was relieved to find Xavier safe at home as his school had closed early. A neighbor had brought him home. As usual, we had lunch and took our daily siesta. The nap helped calm my nerves; I was ready to face the world. We went downtown on the motorcycle to get the car, hoping it would still be there.

And there she was, just as I had left her. We brushed the glass from the front seat and threw out the onions. With my heart racing, I followed Daniel home. During the five-mile drive to our house, I felt vulnerable and exposed. My little white Toyota hatchback felt like a wind tunnel, the hot afternoon air rushing through the openings that once were windows. I felt naked—what if someone threw a rock, or an onion, through the missing front windshield? We drove slowly through the empty, rock-strewn streets, gagging on the black smoke from burning tires. I nodded to the police and army officers patrolling the streets on foot, cradling rifles close to their bodies.

American citizens were notified to leave the country immediately. All family members and non-essential staff of the American diplomatic corps were being evacuated on chartered planes. I didn't want to leave Khartoum; it was my home. As an American, I felt apprehensive. Could I be blamed or harmed because of my nationality? Still, I wanted to stay.

Because I was married to a Belgian, the Belgian embassy issued me a new passport. I carried my new red Belgian passport everywhere I went, the blue American one was stashed away. Thank goodness I had taken five years of French at the Alliance Francaise in Khartoum. Could I speak with a French accent? Or in broken English? I hoped there would be no challenge to my nationality.

Within a few weeks, life was back to normal. Commodity prices stabilized at higher rates. People paid the price and made the necessary sacrifices. I gave back my Belgian passport, and once again, I could live as an American citizen in my adopted country.

President Nimeiry returned from the USA to face the beginning of the end of his regime. Rumor spread that he had made a promise to Allah that if his health improved, he would convert his country to Islam. Indeed, he began a dramatic shift toward an Islamist political government and allied himself with the Muslim Brotherhood. In 1983, he imposed Sharia (Islamic law) throughout the country, alienating both secular Muslims and non-Muslim southerners. Beer, wine, and all other alcoholic drinks were confiscated from stores, clubs, and homes.

In an ostentatious public display, bulldozers pushed thousands of bottles of gin and whiskey into the White Nile. Morality laws were imposed; "attempted adultery" was any woman in a car with a man who wasn't a family member. Many left hands were brutally amputated from supposed thieves. Even Saudi Arabia thought the Sudanese Government had gone too far. Nimeiry was giving Islam a bad name.

After seventeen years of civil war, in 1972, Nimeiry had ended the fighting between the north and south of Sudan. The south, consisting mostly of Christians and animists, was declared a self-governing region. After eleven years of peace, the civil war resumed when Sharia was implemented for the entire country. Many Coptic and other Christian families who had lived in Sudan for generations left the country. The Muslim Brotherhood became a large part of the national government. Finally, in 1985, after sixteen years as president, Mr. Nimeiry was ousted during a military coup and was exiled to Egypt.

Acupuncture Baby

1982–1983

A whisper of discomfort, a twinge, a squeezing cramp, and soon, confirmation. I am not pregnant this month. Again. The sadness, the tears, the disappointment, the sense of failure. I experienced this frustration every month for over three years, yearning for another child.

We'd hoped to have two children close together. But that wasn't to be the case. I was thirty-three years old when Xavier was born. Now I was thirty-six—how much more time did I have?

During our annual visits to California, medical specialists proposed fertility workups. Daniel's tests proved he could be a father again. My medical testing, more extensive, showed nothing wrong with me. Clomid pills to enhance ovulation did not work.

"But I know women who got pregnant after just one time!" Daniel exclaimed.

What I heard was, "What is wrong with you?"

Intimacy took second place to ovulation schedules, morning temperature readings, and various other techniques to increase our prospects of having another child. Nothing worked.

During the cool months of winter, Doctor Wong, an expert in acupuncture, visited Khartoum from Singapore to offer medical services. Several of my friends had received successful treatments for leg cramps, nicotine addiction, and migraine headaches.

"Do you have a treatment for infertility?" I asked him.

"Oh, I learned a procedure during medical school," he grimaced. "I have never tried it in practice. Do you want to be the first?"

"I'll try anything. My doctor in the States said there should be no problems, but nothing has worked. Let's give it a try," I said hopefully, thankful there was another option.

During the next two months, Doctor Wong came to our house several times with his medical bag in hand. Xavier's bedroom became my treatment room. The procedure called moxibustion was timed to my menstrual cycle to stimulate ovulation. While lying on Xavier's bed, I was punctured by needles in various places on my body. Also, small pyramids of "hay," as Doctor Wong called them, were placed over my ovaries and set on fire. The smoldering stacks burned two bright red blisters on my skin. It looked like someone had attacked me with a glowing cigarette. It was painful; the blisters on my skin hurt for a week. How desperate I was to have another child!

Within a month, I knew I was pregnant. Joy, fear, anxiety, relief, happiness!

"Well," said Daniel, "we'll see what this baby looks like," as he pulled on his eyes to mimic Asian features.

It was a difficult pregnancy. Nausea consumed me from conception to delivery. I was tired all the time.

"Chinese women have their baby in the field and keep on working," said Daniel.

"But I'm not Chinese," I retorted, "anyway, that's why so many women die in childbirth—and the babies too." Eating kept nausea at bay; I gained far too much weight.

During our visit to California, when I was in my first trimester, I had a couple of panic attacks. At the base of the Shaver Lake Dam, I feared the cement would break and wash our family away. Later that day, I could not cross the bridge over Stevenson's Creek. I was sure the bridge would collapse with the weight of the car. Daniel stopped the car; Xavier and I got out. Holding hands, keeping my eyes focused on the opposite side, we strolled across the bridge. I heard the roar of rushing spring snowmelt but kept on walking. Safely on the other side, we watched Daniel drive across, and we continued with our excursion.

I was terrified the pregnancy would terminate. I was afraid to do anything that might risk losing this baby. Would have another chance? This baby I yearned for, for so many years.

My doctor in Fresno wanted me to have an ultrasound. The day before the test, I remember telling my mother how worried I was about this unborn child. With a concerned look, she said, "Mothers never stop worrying about their children." I could tell she was worried about me, about the pregnancy, about living in Sudan—most likely about a whole host of things. She was right. Now I know mothers never stop worrying about their children, no matter what age.

The ultrasound looked normal. However, due to my advanced age, my doctor recommended amniocentesis, which itself was a risk. The test couldn't be done until I was twenty weeks into the pregnancy. Daniel returned home as he had to get back to work. Several weeks later, the procedure was performed. The analysis would take several more weeks, so Xavier and I returned home to Khartoum.

The weeks dragged by—weeks of anxiety, worry, and apprehension—as we waited for the results. What if there was a problem? What would I do? I'd gone through so much to get pregnant. Was this my last chance? Fortunately, the report said we were to have a perfect baby girl in March. Relief. Happiness. Glee. A baby girl with a big brother. I wish I had had an older brother. How lucky she will be.

We needed a name suitable in French and English. We paged through the book of names. We started at A—in the Is we found an appropriate name, Isabelle. Our future daughter became Isabelle Marie, Marie for her Belgian grandmother. We all laughed when Xavier sang, "My sister is a bell, ding–ding–ding!"

My nausea continued. I grew bigger along with the baby growing inside me. I didn't sleep well at night, and I was tired all the time. How fortunate that I had a nanny and house servant. I was glad for the pleasant winter weather as the pregnancy progressed. I walked around the neighborhood for thirty minutes every morning and swam every afternoon. However, I looked forward to the due date—nausea, discomfort, and fatigue consumed me. How different this pregnancy was compared to my first! Is it my age? Is it because she's a girl? March twelfth couldn't come soon enough.

On March eleventh, during my morning walk, I tripped over a crack in the sidewalk. Quickly, I grabbed a nearby tree branch; otherwise, I would have fallen. I continued my walk but felt a jarring pain in my back all day. As I got ready for bed that night, my water broke.

"Baby's coming!" I shouted.

Daniel bolted out of bed and darted in all directions.

"Calm down," I said. "She's not going to be born this minute."

He roused Xavier from his sleep and bundled him up. I grabbed the bag I had prepared a week ago. Off we went to the home of our Finnish friends so Xavier could stay with them. Their son Marko went to school with Xavier. They weren't home. Backup plan! Sally and Bob were happy to help.

Daniel raced me to the Khartoum Clinic. It was only two miles away, but I thought he was going to have a heart attack. After being admitted to the clinic, nothing happened. No contractions. One hour later, Daniel went home. I slept all night in the clinic. In the morning, my doctor induced labor because now, baby Isabelle was vulnerable. Dr. Sayda figured when I tripped that morning a toe or foot had scratched the amniotic sack, causing fluid to leak.

Labor started in earnest just a few minutes later, and I wondered why I had been so eager to go through this pain again. I had forgotten what it was like, but it was too late; I could not undo it. The nurses, young women from Ethiopia, massaged my back and feet. I moaned. I thrashed about. I tried to do the relaxation breathing I had practiced at home. I concentrated on the stains blanketing the wall beside me. Reading the book I had brought was out of the question.

"I dreamed of this for years; now it's a nightmare! I've changed my mind. Why, oh why, did I work so hard to get pregnant?" I complained to my doctor.

"It's far too late to change your mind; this baby is on her way out. Relax, don't push yet!" she admonished.

On a sunny afternoon, sixteen hours after we had arrived at the clinic, Isabelle made her appearance. She had a sunny disposition which was reflected in her blue eyes. Her thick, blond hair was so long it covered her ears and neck. Daniel was assured he was her father. She was quiet and lovely, rosy, and perfect. The nausea was over. The pain was forgotten. The extra weight never left.

After three days in the clinic, during which time Isabelle never left my side, Daniel picked us up to take us home—home to our family of four. As we pulled up in front of the house, Daniel turned to me and sweetly asked, "What's for lunch?"

Red Silk and Lederhosen

1983

Veejay loves Gabby. Veejay worked for UNICEF in the town of Wau, a five-hour plane ride from Khartoum. Gabby worked at the Leprosy Clinic there. Veejay was Nepalese, and Gabby was German.

As was the custom at birth in Nepal, Veejay had been promised in marriage to a girl from his parent's village. But Veejay and Gabby fell in love and decide to get married in Wau.

Gabby's parents, from a small Bavarian town in Germany, had never flown before. And yet, they traveled from their home village to an African village to witness the marriage of their daughter. Veejay's parents, ashamed that he had broken his family's wedding promise, disowned him.

Over three days, Daniel made four flights from Khartoum to Wau with wedding guests. Many of the UNICEF families wanted to attend, including our family: me, four-year-old Xavier, and two-week-old Isabelle.

The morning wedding was held in the enormous stone Catholic Cathedral in the center of town. The young African women's choir sang from the heart to celebrate the young couple who did so much for their village. Their buoyant, high-pitched voices filled the vaults of the church. The bride wore a long traditional white lace gown brought from Germany. The groom dressed in a dark suit and tie. Gabby's parents wore traditional German clothing—lederhosen and dirndl.

The afternoon wedding was a traditional Buddhist ceremony. We sat under a red and gold canopy set up under the broad, expansive shade of tropical trees. The perfume of flowers filled the air. Gurung, a fellow Nepalese UNICEF staff member from Khartoum, performed the ceremony. He loved Gabby and Veejay and saw a bright future for the couple. For the afternoon ceremony, the bride dressed in a long red silk brocade dress and colorful headscarf. The groom, in a traditional long white shirt and tight-fitting pants made from the finest cotton, sported a red and gold brocade cap. Many bright colored flower leis adorned them both. Gabby's parents still wore their traditional German clothing. Veejay and Gabby circled the low table alter many times while Gurung sang the customary ceremony.

After the ceremony, their coworkers set up buffet tables. Trays laden with local delicacies of lamb, beans, vegetables, and flatbread were offered to the guests. Tea and cakes concluded the meal. Song and dance lasted throughout the evening.

Beds had been set·up, dormitory-style, in warehouses—one for women and one for men—to accommodate all the visiting UNICEF staff.

Gurung was a very modern man, well-traveled and versed in western ways. He stood in as Veejay's father as well as the priest. He was happy for the couple but sad that Veejay's family had abandoned him. He hoped that one day, they would forgive their son and bring Gabby into their family. I asked Gurung what he would do if his son decided to marry a foreigner.

He froze in place, and solidly announced, "My son would never do such a thing!"

Servants and Slaves

After hiring our first servant, Hilou, in Khartoum North, I was quick to change my opinion about having servants. Servants are not slaves. In many countries, servants have servants. Without domestic employment, many housekeepers wouldn't be able to support themselves or their families. We employed a house servant, a nanny, a gardener, and a man who washed our car. We treated them all with respect and paid a decent wage. I discovered that housework and self-sufficiency have nothing to do with each other. I don't need to be a slave to housework. Even in retirement, I have a housekeeper.

Ahmed, our house servant on Thirty-Seventh Street, was tall, lean, clean, and proud. He never left our home without his shirt ironed and every button in place even though they were mismatched in color and size. Ahmed came from the west near Nyala, where his parents and most of his extended family lived. A strict Muslim, he was honest, caring, and intelligent, although he was illiterate. He knew four words in English: captain, madam, okay, and yes. "No" was not in his vocabulary. Yet, with my limited Arabic and his understanding of his job, we had an excellent working relationship.

He washed the dishes, cleaned the floors, dusted the furniture, and did the laundry. We had the best spaghetti and lasagna in town because I taught him how to make a dough using flour and eggs and run it through the hand-cranked pasta machine. There was only one thing he refused to do. He washed all the household laundry by hand in the bathtub; our clothes, the sheets, the towels. Nonetheless, he wouldn't wash my underwear.

He had several children when we met him and added another one every other year. When his sons were school age, we gave Ahmed a bonus so he could buy school uniforms and supplies. School wasn't mandatory, but a white shirt and blue shorts, plus paper and pencils, were required to attend school. Ahmed was proud his sons would learn to read and write. Now I realize I should have asked about his daughters.

Ahmed and Xavier

Unlike him, Ahmed failed to show up for work. After a week, he arrived one morning to say his wife and newborn baby were in the hospital because the baby was sick. The doctors and nurses were no longer visiting his wife and son; he couldn't understand what was going on. He had had to bring a mattress and sheets for his wife as the hospital didn't provide these. He was also expected to bring food to his wife every day, and that was why he couldn't come to work.

I worked in a clinical laboratory next to the hospital, so I went with him to investigate. We found his wife and baby sharing a bed in an isolation ward. The doctor who was taking care of the baby explained to me that Ahmed's son had been born at home, and, in the traditional ways of Ahmed's tribe, a poultice of mud had been put on the navel to aid healing. Instead, the baby had contracted tetanus from the mud and wasn't expected to live. Therefore, treatment was stopped.

"It's not unusual to see such cases in this hospital," stated the doctor. "The baby didn't respond to our initial treatment. Probably he'll die, as is usually the case."

In spite of the prediction, Ahmed's baby survived and went home. Forty days after his birth, as was the custom, the baby boy was given a name at a party to celebrate his birth. So many babies die shortly after birth that a name isn't given until survival seems likely. I was relieved with this outcome and pleased when Ahmed returned to work.

Every year when we returned from our annual leave, we brought Ahmed a gift. One year we brought him a boom box with radio and cassette player and a year's worth of batteries as he didn't have electricity where he lived. He refused to take it home until we prepared an official document on company stationery stating the boom box was a gift from us. The letter was written in English and Arabic. Ahmed knew if he were found with such a valuable possession, the police would confiscate it, assuming he had stolen it.

It was customary for a family to grant one week vacation with pay for each year a servant worked in a home. After seven years with us, Ahmed wished to take seven weeks off to visit his family in Nyala. He brought a friend, Khalid, who would cover for him during his leave. Khalid was fast, zipping through the dishwashing, dusting, floor mopping, and all the household tasks assigned to him.

Several weeks after Khalid was working for us, we had friends over for dinner. Preparing drinks, we discovered the bottle of gin contained only water. Goodbye, Khalid. Again, I was so happy when Ahmed returned, appreciating him even more.

രജ്ഞോ

Among the several nannies we had over the years, Louisa and Mahalet stand out. Louisa was as homely as she was smart; she spoke five languages. In Eritrea, she had worked as an office manager. But

Daniel, Xavier, Mahalet, and Louisa

fearing for her life, she fled to Sudan, hoping for similar work. She was kind and intuitive, soft-spoken, and always in good humor. She was slight of build and walked with a limp due to a foot deformity. At thirty years of age, she was about ten years older than Mahalet.

Also from Eritrea, Mahalet was beautiful and fresh, a sweet round face, penetrating eyes, and a brilliant smile. I wondered why she was pleasantly plump in a healthy way coming from a country where starvation was rampant. Mahalet could speak English but knew very little about European ways. However, she was quick to learn with Louisa showing her the ropes.

One day we were walking home from a friend's house. A block away from our house, we could hear music floating down the street. As we got closer to home, we realized the blaring music was coming from our stereo system. Running the rest of the way, we dashed into the house to see what was going on. After turning off the music, we checked each room. No one was in the house.

The servants' quarters were on the flat rooftop of our two-story duplex. I climbed the stairs to see if anyone was there. Down on the floor, scrunched into a corner of their little room, was Mahalet, crying and trying to make herself small.

"What's the matter, Mahalet?" I asked.

"Oh, Madam, I'm so sorry. I like to dance and to listen to your music. When I touched some of the buttons on your music, it got too loud. I didn't know what to do. Please don't hurt me. Please forgive me."

I wanted to laugh. However, I did reprimand her for using our things without permission. Later, I showed her how to use our stereo equipment correctly.

One afternoon there was a commotion upstairs. Several times Louisa and Mahalet hurried into our home, grabbing cleaning rags, towels, and buckets of water. Later in the afternoon, uncomfortable with the activity that persisted, I went upstairs to investigate. I almost fainted when I saw a deluge of blood soaking the floor of their room.

Negisti, a servant for our downstairs neighbors, was lying on the bed. When she saw me, she turned her head to the wall. Negisti, a beautiful, elegant young woman, had gotten a job as a domestic in Kuwait. Household duties only? I was doubtful but hoped that was the case. However, when she showed up unwed and pregnant, she was sent back to Khartoum to take care of the situation. Following her back-street abortion, Negisti moved in with Louisa and Mahalet to recuperate. The stay should have been temporary, a couple of days until she was well enough to return to Kuwait; so, they hadn't told me.

Negisti, crying softly, was so weak she couldn't rise from the bed. They were all ashamed. I was afraid of what the outcome could be. I didn't want her to die, and especially, I didn't want her to die at my house. I called my Palestinian friend, Dr. Kattan, to ask if he could help. He said his religious faith prohibited him from fixing a botched abortion. The young women insisted they would be alright.

At 3 a.m., Louisa woke me because Negisti was no longer conscious. I dressed quickly and ran upstairs. We wrapped Negisti's slight body in towels and blankets, carried her down the two flights of stairs, and placed her in the back seat of my car, her head resting in Mahalet's lap. I drove through the empty streets, afraid she would die. Finally, we made it to the public hospital. As they lifted her out of the car, Negisti moaned—I was relieved she was still alive. The two girls carried Negisti to the emergency center. They didn't want me to be involved and said I should go home. I agreed with them on both counts. Three days later, after a D&C and multiple blood transfusions, Negisti came to our house to recover and thank me for saving her life. After a week, she returned to Kuwait.

Both young women left us after a year. Mahalet was accepted as a refugee and immigrated to Wisconsin. She would study English and go to college. She was the only refugee I knew to accomplish this feat. Because she spoke fluent Italian, Louisa got a job in Khartoum as a bookkeeper for an Italian company. Although I was sorry to see them leave us, I was pleased that both women's futures looked bright.

CR&SO

A new nanny would be arriving soon; I needed to inventory the rooms on the roof:
- one string bed called an *angareeb*, made without nails, interlocking legs and frame of rough-hewn wood, thick twine woven in a simple pattern from every side of the frame
- one stool made in the same manner as the bed
- one chest of drawers, standing at an angle due to a missing foot and propped up with a rock

- a dozen nails pounded in the cement wall of the room for hanging clothes
- one charcoal brazier made from a 5-gallon cooking oil tin
- several battered pots and pans, a few plates, a couple of spoons

I hoped Saida would like her new home.

Next to the small concrete all-purpose room was the bathroom with a cold water shower and several pink slivers of soap. A white porcelain squat toilet with footrests, as is usual in Africa, sat next to the shower. Next to the toilet, under a dripping faucet, was a red plastic bucket full of water, a dipping cup floating on top. Water washing in Africa is considered cleaner than using toilet paper. Several towels and men's clothing hung on nails pounded into the wall. I hope Saida doesn't mind sharing the bathroom with Ahmed.

Saida, who came to us when Isabelle was three months old, had worked for a Swiss couple who had three children, one of whom was an infant. They were leaving Khartoum and wished to find a nice family for Saida as she was such a gem with the kids.

Her current family brought Saida, dressed in her Sunday best hand-spun cotton dress typical of her Ethiopian homeland, to our home. Her beautiful dress with a multi-colored border of silk ribbons and embroidery matched the shawl covering her shoulders. She was short and plump, her hair was sprinkled with grey, and her eyes were outlined with kohl. She wore plastic slip-on shoes recently washed— shiny as patent leather. Her brilliant gold earrings and bracelets showed me she wasn't poor. She was introduced to us and demurely offered her hand while looking at the ground. Although she spoke English well, she was a woman of few words. She took Isabelle in her arms, her eyes lit up, and her whole being became like a loving mother. Immediately, I knew this was a good match.

Saida and Isabelle

"Saida, welcome to our home. This is Xavier. He's four years old. And this is Captain Daniel, my husband. He's a pilot, and I work at a hospital. Come upstairs, I'll show you your rooms," I said.

I seized her small suitcase containing all her possessions, and we headed up the stairs to the roof. I was delighted to have her join our household.

I went to work assured Isabelle and Xavier would be loved and mothered in a way different from a real mom. Mothers have many jobs. Saida's job was full attention to the children.

Three days after her arrival, she came to me:

"I have to leave because my uncle is very sick in Ethiopia."

My heart sank. "What? You have to leave us?"

"I must go to visit my uncle."

How did she find out about her uncle in Ethiopia? Refugee grapevine? This can't be true.

After four years of hiring half a dozen young women displaced from Ethiopia and Eritrea, I thought I had someone who would stay. Most of the refugees passing through Khartoum hoped to immigrate to the USA or Europe. Saida was older, mature, and experienced. She didn't want to go to another country. I was heart-broken; I was disappointed. What would I do now? She hadn't lasted a week.

"Will you come back to us after your visit?" I asked, full of hope.

"No, it is very expensive to go there. I won't be able to return," she replied.

How can she afford to visit a sick uncle in a neighboring country? Plane fare is outrageously expensive. No buses cross the border. The civil war between Ethiopia and Eritrea was causing many people to leave. Will she walk in the opposite direction of her countrymen pouring into Sudan? Ethiopia was a dangerous place with gunfire in the markets and bodies in the streets. What was the real issue?

"Don't you like your rooms upstairs? Is Ahmed bothering you?" I asked.

Hanging her head and wringing her hands, she finally whispered, "Madam, I'm afraid of Captain."

Ah ha, Captain Daniel. Yes, he is hot-tempered and loud. When speaking English in his French accent and not understood, he shouted louder, assuming one couldn't hear him. That Mediterranean blood coursing through his veins intimidates me too at times. Loud and brash, his whole being is assuredness and authority. No wonder she is afraid. There is no sick uncle. Maybe this situation was manageable.

We sat down on the couch. I asked Saida to please stay for two weeks, and then we would talk again. I told her Daniel is loud but kind. He had never hurt me or the children, or anyone else for that matter. I said Daniel would never come upstairs, and we could put a lock on her door if she wanted. Two weeks later, we didn't need to have another talk. She came to see he wasn't a dangerous man. Soon she, too, would laugh at his silliness. She never again talked about leaving us.

During her time with us, I saw Saida struggling with needle and thread as she tried to sew a button on her blouse. I realized she didn't see well. I didn't like the thought of her with poor vision in the kitchen using sharp implements, cooking for and feeding Isabelle, and walking in the streets. I took her to the eye doctor to get prescription glasses. She wore them for two days and didn't wear them again.

"Saida, where are your glasses?"

"Oh, madam. Everything is so strange. I don't know where I am when I wear them."

I didn't insist. Saida was comfortable in her vision of the world. Things aren't always what they seem.

Coffee Day

The rich aroma of coffee descended the stairwell of our home, triggering memories of companionship and indulgence.

It must have been Wednesday or Saturday, the two days each week Saida made coffee. She started with green coffee beans grown in the Ethiopian mountains and then toiled for over an hour to produce a few sips of the hot, sweet, delicious drink.

As the story goes, an Ethiopian goatherd discovered the magical properties of coffee beans when he noticed his goats romped around, kicking up their heels, after they ate the bright red berries from a wild bush. The goats became so energized they would not sleep at night. The goatherd reported this to the abbot of a monastery who then made a drink from the berries. Much to his delight, he found he stayed alert through the long hours of evening prayer. Knowledge of the stimulating fruit began to spread in the region. Thus, coffee started its journey around the globe.

Caffeine! The most widely used stimulant in the world. Today coffee grows in many tropical countries. However, all coffee plants trace their heritage to the ancient coffee forests in the high plateaus of Ethiopia. Frisky, energetic goats discovered the drug of choice from boardroom CEOs to midnight shift workers.

Khartoum, with its diaspora of Ethiopian refugees, supported a market for green coffee beans from the mountains east of Sudan. Saida bought her beans in a dusty corner market in Khartoum II. On coffee days, she began her preparations early in the morning, carefully inspecting each bean to make sure there were no blemishes. She washed enough beans for a pot of coffee then placed them in a shallow basket to dry all afternoon in the hot African sun.

Around three o'clock in the afternoon, sitting on a small stool next to her room on the roof, she lit the charcoal in her tin brazier. She spread out the green beans in a single layer in her small, dented aluminum frying pan. When the coals were hot, she began the roasting. To keep the beans from burning, Saida shook the pan and stirred the beans with a wooden stick to assure each one, top and bottom, came in contact with the heat. The beans crackled and popped as they began to roast. Just as the oils started to emerge from the beans, the distinctive fragrance of freshly roasted coffee permeated the rooftop and floated downstairs to my house.

Saida was an expert roaster and knew the exact moment when the roasting was complete—a few seconds longer and the beans would burn, a few seconds too soon and the flavor would not be optimal. She removed the pan from the coals so the beans could cool.

In the fifteenth century, coffee had spread to the Arabian Peninsula, northeast of Ethiopia. Coffee houses became a popular place for men to gather and socialize. Often referred to as Schools of the Wise, coffee houses became an important center for the exchange of information. This tradition still exists today in the Middle East and, more recently, at Starbucks throughout the world.

Next, Saida added the fresh-roasted, dark-brown beans to a wooden mortar. She crushed the brittle beans into a coarse powder, the pestle hitting the sides of the mortar in a steady rhythm.

As thousands of pilgrims from all over the world visited the holy city of Mecca, the Wine of Araby, as the drink was called, spread far beyond Arabia.

Saida rolled a piece of cardboard to create a funnel and added the grounds down the long, narrow spout into the *jebena*, a coffee pot made of tin or clay. The pot, rounded on the bottom, sat on a beaded donut-shaped ring designed especially for it. Next, she added water, then nestled the *jebena* into the lumpy hot coals in the brazier.

When coffee reached Europe in the seventeenth century, it was called Satan's drink because it was so popular in the Muslim world. Pope Clement VIII was asked to ban the drink. He thought he should try it before he proclaimed it sinful. On the contrary, he enjoyed the coffee so much he blessed it, and soon it spread all over Europe. Coffee houses became the center of the European social and political scene. King Charles II of England tried unsuccessfully to ban coffee because of its intellectually stimulating properties. He feared political dissent originating in the coffee houses would result in his dethronement.

As the coffee brewed, Saida filled our tiny cups halfway with sugar. When steam began to escape from the pot, Saida removed the pot from the coals. A thick plug of loofah was added to the neck of the spout; this prevented the grounds from boiling over. The grounds were allowed to settle, and then the pot was placed back in the coals. Three times the coffee came to a boil and was removed at the precise moment. The coffee had now reached maximum flavor. The grounds settled in the pot placed at an angle in the donut-shaped holder.

After a few minutes, she poured the rich, clear liquid extract in a continuous flow over the small cups. Stopping the flow would disturb the coffee grounds in the pot. The coffee was stirred with a little stick to dissolve the sugar. Any grounds were allowed to settle in the cup. I was honored when Saida invited me to share the Wine of Araby with her.

Saida and I carefully lifted the petite hot cups to our noses. As though I was inhaling the fragrance of fine wine, I savored the aroma as my taste buds got ready for the two sips of the hot, sweet, delicious drink.

A Day in My Life

Six a.m. Already heat streamed through the living room windows. The sun began its daily journey half an hour ago. I started my day with a shower to rinse off the sweat from the hot night's sleep. The power went out in the middle of the night. The air cooler shut down. The bedroom temperature rose to 90° within minutes. April was the hottest month of the year—temperatures hovered around 110°. Over half the year the temperature was above 100° every day. At least that is how I remember it!

Daniel got up while I made breakfast of eggs, toast, and fruit. Six-year-old Xavier got himself up and ready for school. I put Isabelle in her highchair. We all had breakfast together.

"Good morning, madam, captain," greeted Saida as she let herself into the house, rushing over to pick up Isabelle and balance her on her hip. She would get Isabelle ready for the day, then clean the breakfast dishes.

Daniel headed off to the UNICEF office on his motorcycle.

"Bye, kiddos. Love you," I said, giving the kids a kiss and a hug. I headed downstairs and drove to my office at the Stack Lab downtown.

Xavier was picked up for French school by our neighbor, Mr. Mohamed. He and his wife, Muna, had twin boys in Xavier's class, Farook and Fahid. The family, from Tunisia, spoke only Arabic and French. Xavier played with the boys after school and spoke Arabic better than I did.

Isabelle spent three mornings a week at Susan's home, an American whose husband worked at the U.S. embassy. Susan had a two-year-old daughter and had formed a small playgroup for several youngsters. They would sing, paint, and learn to share. Isabelle loved it so much that she waited at our front door, expecting to be picked up even on the days there was no school.

Ahmed arrived soon after I left for work. As he did every day, he started with the laundry then hung it out on the patio to dry. After four years of washing clothes in the bathtub, he was grateful when we imported a small automatic washing machine. After twenty minutes on the patio, the clothes were dry, and he commenced with the ironing. Next, he removed the layer of dust that accumulated on the furniture overnight, so thick one could write one's name in it. He made the beds, cleaned the bathrooms, and then washed the tile floors. The household would be in order when I arrived home from work early afternoon. If I had been to the central market that morning, Ahmed would trim the meat, clean the fruits and vegetables, and put everything in the refrigerator.

When the Nile flooded in the summer months, the water from the faucets looked like chocolate milk. The hydroelectric plants on the rivers, clogged with silt and debris, struggled to provide the city with electricity and water during the hottest time of the year. Consequently, we experienced frequent power outages and low water pressure, sometimes lasting for days. Our five kVA generator on the roof and the booster pump on the water line at the base of the house provided us with these basic necessities during power cuts. Ahmed filtered the "chocolate milk" through our two-gallon Katadyn filter, so we had clear, clean drinking water. However, our dishes and clothes, as well as our bodies, retained some of the nutrient-rich minerals from the river.

CRSO

Every Thursday, I awoke before daybreak to get to the central market at sunrise when the produce was still fresh from the farms. The city market consisted of several open-air buildings. The merchants sold nothing in packages or tins; everything was fresh. As the sun rose, bringing light but not yet heat, the market was abuzz with vendors calling out to potential customers. Bargaining in Arabic with the sellers helped me get the best prices.

Christmas 1984

I approached the market, empty shopping baskets in hand, and was surrounded by young boys pushing and shoving to get my attention.

"Madam, I am strong."

"Madam, I helped you last week."

I selected one who would carry my baskets soon to be laden with the produce from the banks of the Nile. The hot, dry climate meant that year-round, the market provided an abundance of diverse fresh food.

Zucchini, tomatoes, onions, and garlic would make a delicious ratatouille. Eggplant for a tasty babaganoush. Peppers and okra would be added to a stew. Cucumbers, mixed with yogurt, made a refreshing salad. Leaves from a jute-like plant would be cooked into *mulukhiyah*—a slimy mess that was both nutritious and delicious. Bananas, mangoes, and watermelons would make a nice fruit salad. Cooked guavas were yummy with yogurt. Citrus was always in abundance; sweet grapefruit almost the size of volleyballs, oranges with green skin, and the ubiquitous limes. As most vendors did not have a scale, produce was sold by the group; a stack of four tomatoes, a pile of three eggplants, a mound of zucchini.

In the cool winter weather, I could buy cantaloupe, cabbage, broccoli, and lettuce. We welcomed the change in our diet.

The last stop was the meat bazaar. Carcasses of beef and lamb, fresh from the slaughterhouse, were being off-loaded from the trunks of taxis. Hearts, livers, lungs, and unidentifiable animal parts were laid out on the scuffed wooden counters. Butchers hacked off hunks from the sides of meat swinging on hooks.

Potential buyers carefully inspected live chickens and rabbits. The chosen were quickly processed, ready for the stew pot. Nile perch were gutted and readied for the frying pan. Beef in Sudan must be cooked for many hours over low heat; cattle that walk across the desert to market are very tough. However, the choice part of beef, the whole filet, was sold separately. Baskets full of this high-quality, most expensive, tender meat were paraded in front of me. I chose two or three of the freshest looking pieces.

The market was a busy place. My arrival at sunrise meant I avoided not only the crowds of men shopping for their families but also the flies that held conventions on the slabs of meat as the day progressed from cool to sweltering hot.

CR♥O

After my five hour workday, I left the office about 1 p.m. When I stepped outside the air-conditioned laboratory, the sun beat me down. The heat was oppressive. Took my breath away. I felt shorter. I climbed into my clean Toyota hatchback—Yousef had washed it as he did every day. I wished it had air conditioning. The drive home seemed longer than the morning commute.

At home, I greeted the children already home from school and then headed off to the kitchen to prepare lunch, our main meal of the day. The air-cooler in the living room provided little comfort in the hot kitchen. I preferred to do our own cooking but appreciated the prep work Saida had done. Daniel would be home just after two o'clock; everything would be ready for our meal. When we finished eating, Daniel called to Ahmed to prepare his coffee. Ahmed cleared the table, washed and dried the dishes while I got the kids ready for their nap.

Siesta was not only for the little ones. After finishing his coffee, Daniel and I would head off for our nap. Our bed was placed directly in line with the air cooler. Relief. Maybe it was 85°—so much cooler than the kitchen.

An hour or so later, revived, we headed to the American Club. The sun was low in the late afternoon sky. A swim in the pool cooled me to the core. Xavier was a good swimmer, having learned when he was six months old. Daniel swam with him while I stayed close to Isabelle, either in the kiddie pool or in the big one. She also learned to swim before she could walk. We met many friends and families also looking for relief from the heat. Usually, we had a light dinner at the club.

If Daniel were flying the next day, he would want to go home for our simple evening meal. Daniel would sit down in front of the air-cooler and read a book. He insisted the house be quiet, that he not be disturbed.

I read the kids a story. Quietly, we picked up the toys scattered around their bedroom. I got the kids ready for bed and closed up the house for the night. Daniel would arise at 3 a.m. to get out the door by 4 a.m. and make his way to the airport to prepare for his flight.

"If I am not focused, I could kill a dozen United Nations staff, including myself. *Oui,* my job has more responsibility than a doctor who only kills one person at a time!" he declared.

For the second time that day, I took a shower, then headed to bed, book in hand. Nine p.m., the sun had set three hours ago, bringing some relief from the heat.

In many ways, life was easy. Overall, life was a challenge.

Hotel Sandwich

1985

The worst year of my life began with bad news on January 1, 1985. I got out of bed and noticed my eyes were yellow. Also, my urine was the color of Pepsi Cola. Having analyzed thousands of urine samples in the clinical laboratory, I knew what it meant. I had hepatitis!

The Meridian Hotel had opened its doors several years prior, the first luxury hotel in the country. The beautiful eight-story building, a block from my office, opened with luxurious décor in the lobby, unlike anything else in Khartoum. The elite, wealthy residents now had a French restaurant in which to indulge on cordon bleu, crepes, and mousse au chocolat.

The hotel opened a small take-out sandwich shop facing El Qasr Avenue. It served chicken and beef shawarma. The seasoned meat, stacked on a vertical spit topped with an onion and tomato, turned slowly as it cooked. Then, the meat, roasted to perfection, was expertly sliced with a sharp knife into a French baguette and topped with fresh greens from the market. Because this shop was located close to my office, I occasionally treated myself to this delightful sandwich.

One night, a couple of days after I had eaten a sandwich from that shop, I awoke and felt I had been poisoned. I repeatedly purged my gut from both ends. I expected my GI tract would turn inside out. I felt green and weak. I thought I might die.

Daniel was in the south of Sudan for a couple of nights. I was alone with the children. Oh, when will this stop! Please let me live until morning!

When Saida came into the house at 7 a.m., I had her phone my colleague, Dr. Mamoun, my physician and friend. He came to the house right away and, after a brief exam, proclaimed I would live and would be fine in a few days. Food poisoning was the culprit.

About three weeks later, I developed a constant headache. Tylenol helped for a couple of days. When I complained about it getting worse, my colleague, Suad, gave me something stronger. I don't know what it was, but it helped ease the pain for a few more days. However, on December 31, I felt lousy and left work early so I could rest before going out for New Year's Eve celebrations. I didn't get out of bed for two months.

On New Year's Day, Dr. Mamoun, once again, came to our home and confirmed my suspicions—hepatitis! With such a severe illness, my friends expected me to go home to California. Bed rest was the treatment. I knew I would get more rest at my home in Khartoum. Furthermore, I couldn't face multiple plane flights across three continents. It was winter; the weather was perfect in Khartoum. I didn't want to take Xavier out of school. I had servants to take care of me, the children, and the house.

Blood tests later confirmed I had Hepatitis A. By May, I was strong enough to go back to work; however, it took a full year to recover. I still feel tainted—I'm rejected as a blood donor forever because of that illness.

Looking back, I suspect both illnesses came from one delicious lunch from the Meridian sandwich shop. I can still picture a young man with filthy hands stuffing the fresh greens into my baguette. Do you think I ever went back to that sandwich shop? With the fresh crusty bread and tasty, tender roasted meat?

Three Days in August

1985

"**M**ama, don't leave me!" Xavier called out as the surgery team rushed his gurney down the hallway of the University Medical Center in Fresno. The double doors slammed shut. My life changed forever!

Tuesday, August 13, started like any other day. We were in California on our annual visit. I had a medical appointment that morning, so my mom took Xavier and Isabelle to the park. When I got home, my sister Charlotte joined us for lunch.

As we cleared the table after eating, Xavier said, "I'm going to ride my bike and then come back for my cookie."

Daniel had flown home to Khartoum the day before. The kids and I would stay with my parents for another week to finish our shopping. We would buy clothing, shoes, and toys—things we couldn't buy in Sudan.

The doorbell rang. We expected someone to open the screen door and walk in as family and neighbors did so often in the summer. The doorbell rang again. I approached the entry door and saw a boy I didn't know.

When he saw me, he shouted, "Xavier's been hit by a truck!"

Dropping everything, I sprinted out the door. Across the street in our quiet neighborhood, a city garbage truck was parked at the curb.

I followed the boy as he ran across the street. We dashed around the truck, engine revving, and there he was. My son—three weeks shy of his seventh birthday—blond hair brushing his eyelids—lying in the grass under the pink-blossomed crepe myrtle tree.

"My leg hurts," he said as I bent down to support his torso. I didn't notice the bone fragments in the grass nor the blood flowing down the curb.

"Maybe you broke your leg," I said as I eyed his crumpled bike under the truck—the old bicycle his grandfather had lovingly painted a few weeks before our arrival.

"I've called an ambulance. It should be here in a few minutes," said the driver of the garbage truck in a trembling voice. In moments, I heard sirens.

Xavier looked fine, only his leg hurt. His T-shirt and shorts were clean. He couldn't be severely injured. The little blue bicycle was mangled beyond repair, but not my son.

I thought, "Maybe we don't need an ambulance; perhaps it's just his leg." He still had his shoes on.

An ambulance screeched to a halt; a police motorcycle pulled up to the curb; a small crowd of neighbors had gathered. The Emergency Medical Technicians (EMT) got to work right away. They cut off his shorts. I saw muscles and bones, a body torn open. A support board was slipped under his hips; a pressure suit was wrapped around his torso and legs. The EMT rushed him to the back of the ambulance. I jumped into the front seat. We were on our way to the trauma center.

Time slowed down. Sirens blaring. Red lights flashing. Cars pulling over. We ran through red lights. What are they doing to him back there? I can hear him talking. Maybe it's not so bad. The ambulance driver didn't speak to me. Is that a bad sign? Can't he reassure me? What is he thinking? Please tell me everything will be all right. A thousand thoughts churned through my mind. I felt stunned and helpless.

The trauma team met the ambulance outside the hospital, and Xavier was whisked off to a treatment area. I was directed to the registration desk. How can you ask me all these questions? My little boy is hurt! He needs me beside him; I need to be with him. I had trouble answering their questions; details of names, addresses, insurance, too much information; my mind was elsewhere. After we finished the registration, I was told to wait. Someone would call me when I could see him.

In a daze, I sat down and immediately realized I needed to use the restroom. Odd how the body reacts when in shock—my bowels purged to the point of hollowness. I was surprised to see my knees and shins covered in blood. My son's blood. He must have bled into the grass where I knelt beside him. I got paper towels and cleaned up as best I could in a hospital restroom. Other women stared at me. I felt like I needed to explain, but words would not form in my mind. I returned to the waiting room and saw my mother, sister, and father there. Why was my father here? He was supposed to be at work. They must think this is bad.

Is death at the door? Don't open it. It's a mistake. Find the old, the sick, the ones in pain. My son is young and healthy. Go away.

Within a short time, I was called into the treatment area. And there he was, my healthy son who said he would ride his bike and then come back for a cookie. That is how the day was to proceed. But we're in a trauma center.

"Mama, I need to go to the toilet," he whispered to me.

"Nurse, he needs a urinal."

Instead, they inserted a catheter. Bright red, bloody urine filled the tube! Oh no...he is hurt—hurt real bad. He has more than a broken leg.

A doctor explained to me Xavier's hip was broken. They needed to go to surgery and pin it back together. They would fix him up. Good as new? He had lost a lot of blood; in fact, he had no pulse when the

114

EMT first checked him. However, plasma and other fluids were being pumped into him.

Within an hour—was time standing still—we were rushing down the hallway to the surgery suite. My son was coherent and lucid, a little boy asking his mother not to leave him.

Xavier's hip bone was shattered. The damage was so extensive they were unable to repair it. They did what they could to stop the bleeding. When he was medically stable, they would fix his hip. I didn't hear what they wouldn't tell me.

"Will he be able to run? To play soccer? Would he be able to walk? Should I have my husband come back to Fresno?" So many questions, yet, I couldn't ask the one I needed to ask, "Will he live?"

My mind raced. Change of plans. How long will he be in the hospital? What about rehab? When will we be able to go home to Sudan? What about my work in the research lab? Will we ever go back? One day at a time, one hour at a time, one minute at a time. Just get through the next few seconds.

In Khartoum, Daniel had arrived home only hours before I called. Unlike most people in Sudan, we had a telephone in our house; and, it worked some of the time. Imagine my surprise when I called Daniel from the hospital payphone, and he answered. I told him the doctor said he should come as soon as possible. He was on the next plane.

It was late night. Surgery was over. Xavier was wheeled into intensive care. My family went home. The head nurse prepared a bed for me in her office. I slept.

Wednesday morning, I awoke to smiling faces. Xavier's nurses said he was alert and trying to say "Mama." I rushed to his bedside. There was my lovely son surround by charts and monitors, tubes from every orifice, beeping bleeping machines telling me he was alive. His eyes were closed. He seemed agitated—did the nurses really think he was alert? Even though he had a respirator in his mouth, his lips moved; nonetheless, no sound came out. I hoped he was saying

"Mama." I hadn't left him. He was alive. The worst was over. He was healing.

It was a busy day. My brother, Jeff, who was out of town when the accident occurred, arrived at the hospital. Tears rolled down his cheeks as he hugged me tightly. The ambulance drivers came by with a lollipop bouquet. The garbage truck driver came with his wife and children. Family, friends, and neighbors came to the hospital. Mom brought me personal items and clean clothes. In the heat of the August summer, I walked around the block of the hospital several times to breathe fresh air, to get some exercise, to have quiet time. Thinking positively. Filling my mind with healing thoughts. Coming to grips with reality. This was not a nightmare. This was real.

I was at Xavier's bedside when allowed, holding his hand, telling him about soccer games he would play, judo tournaments he would win, thinking he may walk with a limp, picturing him alive.

My sister was with me in the evening when a Code Blue was announced over the loudspeaker. It was Xavier's room!!! Having worked in a hospital for many years, I knew there was a significant problem.

He was bleeding. Back to surgery. Patch him up as best they could.

The next day, Thursday, was the turning point. His organs began to fail. Blood was pumped into him as fast as it left his little body. He went through ninety-eight units of blood—his body held only four units at a time. A public service announcement on TV and radio stated there was a critical need for type O blood in the community—blood for my son.

Unresponsive. Monitors continued to beep. Xavier fought the fight until his father arrived in the evening. In the wee hours of Friday morning, his body had had enough. His little heart, so full of love and life a few days before, stopped beating. The doctor opened his chest and massaged the inert organ. It didn't respond. Emerging from the

116

treatment room in tears, the doctor told us there was nothing more to do. Our little boy was gone.

We asked to be with him. His body was still warm. It was quiet except for our hushed sobs. He was alive only in our hearts. I hadn't left him.

It was 3 a.m. The charge nurse said she would drive us home. Had she stayed past her shift, knowing she would be needed? Her old beat-up car was full of junk food wrappers. Nevertheless, I felt her kindness and sympathy, although no words were spoken. A million thoughts in my head. My plans and dreams of our family's future came undone.

Taking the first steps in my new life, I rang the doorbell of my parent's home. He's gone. Death had opened the door. I became the mother of a dead child. How many parents belong to that club? I wanted to shout out—the order is wrong, parents die before their children. I am in shock, can't hold a thought. Tell me what to do; darkness surrounds me. Pain washes over me like a scalding shower. Turn it off. Sleep is out of the question.

Funeral planning takes one's mind off the tragedy for a moment. Who will do what, do you want this, shall we do that? My son is dead. It doesn't matter.

Do you need a prescription to help you sleep? Dad said yes. I said no. I needed to feel the pain. Make the calls. Write letters to friends all over the world.

Isabelle, always happy and serene, was playing in the middle of the living room. Suddenly she screamed as if a snake had bitten her. Did she know? Could she feel our pain? How do you tell a two-year-old her big brother is dead?

How can life go on as usual for everyone else? I want to howl to the world, "My son is dead!" See those kids playing over there? Why didn't this happen to them? Why me? Why him? If only he had eaten his cookie, would we have averted this tragedy? If only this, if only that. Can't change it. My son is dead.

Life goes on. Isabelle needs me. I must be strong for her. My heart died a little that day. What if this happens to her? Sealing myself off to prevent more pain. I must be strong for everyone else who isn't doing so well. I learned a lesson I did not need to know—I am a survivor. Go ahead, throw it at me. I can weather any storm. If I can endure the death of my child, I can survive anything. If pain teaches us who we are, I was learning too much.

The funeral. Greet friends and family. Be polite when told God needs Xavier in his garden. Or he is in a better place. Or it was his time. None of it makes sense. However, saying anything is better than saying nothing. He should be here with us. He was only six years old. His front teeth were beginning to emerge, teeth he needed as an adult.

Two weeks later, on our way home to Khartoum, we stopped in Belgium to spend several days with Daniel's parents. The mood was black. We walked on eggshells. Daniel began his descent into guilt. He felt God was punishing him for all the bad things he had done in his life. However, he couldn't understand why I had to suffer too. Therefore the guilt was doubled.

Thus began the first steps towards divorce. I was the pillar. I was the strength. I must ease their pain. I must create a new future for us all. In profound sadness, we talked about the good times with Xavier.

His Belgian grandparents recalled their last view of him at the airport several weeks earlier. His little arm vigorously waved goodbye to them as they stood behind the glass viewing windows—their first grandchild, their only grandson.

Back home in Khartoum, everything was the same; yet, nothing was the same. What to do with his toys? His clothes? How to tell the neighbors? The school? Our work colleagues? Who knows? Who doesn't know? People are uncomfortable. Don't know what to say. The worst thing is to say nothing. Do you know? Do you care? A simple "I am sorry" or "I don't know what to say" is better than saying nothing.

Famine was still raging in Ethiopia. Pictures of starving children—big heads, ribs protruding, stomachs distended—blanketed the news. My heart went out to the thousands of families experiencing the death of a child. However, death all around does not make it easier. Their suffering filled my heart, the pain of grieving mothers.

Since Daniel is Catholic and Xavier was baptized in the Catholic Church in Khartoum, we had a memorial service there. Our Sudan family—Christians, Muslims, Buddhists, and Hindus—came to share our sorrow. It eased my heart.

About six weeks later, I felt different. I was no longer in shock. I had changed physically and emotionally. Finally, I knew there was no answer to "Why me?" There was no undoing the "If only..." I felt more like the old me, although I would never be the same. Was I the mother of two or one? When asked, "how many children do you have," do I need to tell the truth? I say I have one daughter, one beautiful daughter.

A couple of months later, Dr. Anwara came to my work. Xavier had been playmates with her son, Mohammed, as they were close in age. With tears rolling down my cheeks, I told her what had happened.

When did this occur?" she asked me.

"It was in the middle of August when we were in California," I replied.

Imagine my surprise when she calmly responded, "that was over 40 days ago! Why are you still crying?"

Muslims families mourn dramatically, crying and wailing for forty days. Then life goes on. Maybe we have it wrong. Had I mourned my loss? Had I cried enough? Had I grieved?

Anniversaries come and go. Do I remind people? Would it bring back the pain and sorrow to those who knew him? Or can we remember the joy? He is not gone; he is a part of who I am. His memory, a happy one now, lives in me, and so many others he touched. A decade later, I forgot August 16 was a noteworthy date. I can say now with a smile through my tears, "I am happy he was with us for a short time, rather than not at all."

Xavier—my first pregnancy, my firstborn. A delightful baby. A happy child; curious, mischievous, athletic, strong-willed, polylingual; indeed, an international child. So much potential. For too short a time in this incarnation.

"You still live in my heart; I didn't leave you."

Xavier - the day before the accident

Last photo - family of four

The Daily Journey

1986

Hand in hand, they set off on their daily journey. The wrinkled, calloused brown hand firmly grasped the small, flawless, white hand.

"Come, little *bent,* it's time to go," said Saida. "Get your shoes on."

"Bye-bye, Mama." three-year-old Isabelle shouted as she ran to find her flip-flops.

Saida, also in flip-flops, was dressed in a long flowing skirt with a tattered hem, a goofy T-shirt with a logo she couldn't read, and a home-spun cotton shawl covering her head and shoulders. In the other hand, she carried a dented aluminum pail with a lid that rattled with every step. Isabelle—her long blond pigtails swinging side to side—and Saida set off for their afternoon adventure through the neighborhood. Turning right at the garden gate, they crossed the pot-holed street that once was paved; but weather, time, and neglect had taken their toll. With every step, they left footprints in the dust.

"Salaam alaykum," shouted Mohammed from the doorway of the neighborhood souk on the corner. He was standing in front of metal racks with a few dust-covered packages of cookies made in Egypt, boxes of tea from India, and several cello-wrapped toys from China faded to an indistinguishable color.

"Wa 'alaykum as-salaam," responded Saida, *"Inta quayse?"*

"Al-Hamdu lillah," replied Mohammed, bowing slightly as he handed a cold Pepsi to a young lad at the counter. Greetings exchanged, Saida and Isabelle continued down the cracked, uneven sidewalk towards their destination.

Another right turn, a stroll to midblock, and they arrived. By the time the farmer drove up in his faded-green pickup truck, twenty to thirty people were waiting. Most were household servants or nannies. Like Saida, many brought their young charges with them. All were waiting to collect fresh milk still warm from the cow.

When the farmer arrived, a dozen milk cans clattering in the bed of his truck, everyone assembled into a formal line to await their turn. They respected the order in which they had arrived. After the two measured scoops were carefully poured into our aluminum pail, Isabelle and Saida began the short trek home.

At home, Saida poured the milk through a sieve to filter out any cow hair; then, she heated the milk just to boiling. Of course, it wasn't pasteurized, but it seemed like a good thing to do. When cool, the milk was put into a glass jar and placed in the refrigerator. By morning the luscious, velvety-smooth cream had risen to the top. I carefully scooped up the cream and added it to the previous collections in the freezer. When there was enough, we would make ice cream. Slightly thawed and whipped with a little sugar and vanilla, it was a special treat. Some days we set a bowl of milk, with a bit of starter, on the patio. The warmth of the sun transformed it into yogurt.

"Saida, why do you leave at 3 o'clock? The milk isn't delivered until after 4 p.m." I asked.

"Oh, madam, there is never enough milk for everyone, so I want to make sure we get our share," she replied.

That made sense, we paid a monthly fee, and the milk was distributed until there was no more. Dairy cows produce different amounts of milk each day, and sometimes there was not enough for everyone. Sometimes, the latecomers went home with empty pails.

One day I had to collect Isabelle because they hadn't arrived back home when expected. I saw right away why Saida left so early. Waiting for the milk was a social event. The nannies stood in groups exchanging the latest gossip under the shade of the few tall trees. Also, I saw Isabelle enjoyed playing with the other kids.

Fresh milk wasn't sold in stores. One could buy tins of powdered milk made somewhere in the world by Nestle. Sometimes cardboard cartons of UHT (Ultra High Temperature) milk could be found in stores. It seemed bizarre to buy milk that had sat for months on a hot, dusty shelf.

Before our neighborhood farmer began selling milk, we purchased fresh milk from the donkey-man. He roamed the neighborhoods shouting, "*Leben, leben, leben,*" as he trotted down each street. Two large tin milk cans were carefully balanced on the neck of his donkey. Hearing his cries, Saida would dash down to the road with her pail to buy some milk. The man, dressed in his stained, ragged *jelabiya*, his formerly white headdress always needing adjustment, was precariously perched on the donkey's rear end, his legs crossed over the donkey's back. Somehow keeping his flip-flops on, he expertly hopped off, hitting the ground ready to measure out the desired quantity of *leben*. The sieving of this milk revealed more than a few cow hairs. Sand, leaves, and other debris removed, the milk was fresh and delicious.

This was my initial experience of farm to table before the expression even existed.

Blue Nile

Drink from the Nile I did—every time I plunged into the river, tumbling off water skis or toppling from my windsurf board.

Nine hundred miles away in the Ethiopian highlands, the seasonal rains gather over Lake Tana, the origin of the Blue Nile. Rushing over rocks and plunging down crevices and canyons, it collects smaller tributaries along its journey from the mountains then eases onto the flat desert plains of eastern Sudan. The Blue Nile brings water and nutrients to the cotton, peanuts, and other crops that flourish when the floods cease.

Our little group of ex-pats also flourished in the Blue Nile. Outside of the annual flood season, the cool weather and sunshine from November to March meant it was picnic time. Our winter treks to the river offered a respite from the hardships of life in Khartoum. We loaded our supplies into the trunk of the car and joined our caravan of friends. Off we went, fifteen miles south of Khartoum, to our favorite unnamed island in the middle of the river exposed when the flooding ceased.

Although shorter than the White Nile, the Blue Nile contributes about seventy-five percent of the water to the Nile proper.

We chose the Blue Nile for swimming as it was free of the parasite that causes Bilharzia (Schistosomiasis). Prevalent in the White Nile, the larvae burrow through human skin, causing acute and chronic illnesses. Besides, crocodiles hadn't been seen in the Blue Nile for years.

"Did you bring beer?" I asked my Canadian friend, Sally. "We just bottled some red wine; I brought two bottles to share." Alcoholic drinks had been banned with the implementation of Sharia in 1983. At considerable risk, we were brewing our own spirits from kits purchased in London.

"Isabelle, let's get your life vest on," I commanded as we transferred our lunches, umbrellas, and kids into a rubber raft.

Daniel struggled to unload the windsurf board from the top of the car so he could sail it to the island.

"Do you have room for Jonah in the raft? Nathaniel and Adam will swim with me," said Charlotte, my Danish friend.

"Well, the raft is pretty full, how about waiting for the second trip?" I replied.

The ancient fable about how to transport a fox, a goose, and a basket of grain across a river came to mind as we couldn't leave anything unattended on either the river bank or the island. The curious Sudanese kids from the nearby farms found our possessions alluring and inviting.

We set off swimming, pulling the cords of the raft filled with our precious cargo of kids, food, and drinks towards the island's sandy beach. Frantz and Helen would arrive later in their powerboat, bringing family, food, and water skis.

The White Nile, the sister river of the Blue, bubbles out of the ground in Rwanda then pours into Lake Victoria in Tanzania heading north. Leaving the lake over Ripon Falls in Uganda, it meets the flat plains in the south of Sudan. There it forms the Sudd, a slow, shallow swamp, two hundred miles wide and two hundred and fifty miles long, ten times larger than the Florida Everglades. Near the town of Malakal, it once again becomes a river.

The White Nile meets the Blue Nile in Khartoum in front of the Presidential Palace. During the winter months, the wide lazy rivers—one clear blue-green, the other silty gray—gently kiss and eventually

126

merge, forming the Nile River, the longest river in the world. On its 4,200 mile journey through eleven countries, the river collects nutrient-rich silt and deposit the sediment along the thousands of miles then finally drains into the Mediterranean Sea.

"I can't believe it's minus five degrees in East Lansing, Michigan," said Jeff, the administrator for the tropical disease research project where I worked. "Yesterday, when I left, it was snowing so hard I thought my flight would be canceled."

However, here he is, on the beach of an island in the middle of the Blue Nile. Seventy degrees, bright sunny skies—we love the winter weather in Khartoum. The river water was fresh and clear. The lazy current meant one could swim upstream and not move far from our picnic site. The wide sandy beaches were scrubbed clean by the annual floods providing a playground for the kids to run, jump, and build sandcastles. The soft breeze was cool, strong enough to keep the sail of the windsurf up but gentle enough for a novice surfboarder to think she was a pro.

Dozens of black kites, large European raptors, having migrated to Sudan for the winter, were gliding and cawing overhead. Roosters crowed from the nearby farms. Cows and goats, herded by the farmers' children, stumbled down the steep river bank for their afternoon drink—their grunts, groans, and bleating reached us across the water. As the animals drank, the young herders stared at the foreigners cavorting on the island. Sudanese underwear covers most of the body. Wearing only our bathing suits, I suppose we were considered naked. In fact, the Sears catalog was banned at the airport customs considered pornographic because of the pictures of people in underwear.

One afternoon, across from our island, three young men brought several top-dollar racehorses to the river to drink and bathe. As the horses swam along the edge of the river, one young man rode his horse too far into the water. The rider didn't realize his weight pushed the horse underwater. They got caught in the current. The horse gasped for

Picnic on the Blue Nile

air and screamed hysterically every time it surfaced. Frantz took off in his powerboat to try to save them. Everyone was now in a panic. The young man couldn't swim and was afraid to let go of the horse's mane. The horse, kicking wildly, was trying to keep its head above water. Not wanting to get too close to the thrashing horse, Franz threw a rope to the young man and pulled him into the boat, saving his life. Unfortunately, the exhausted horse wasn't so lucky. The racehorse was worth more than all those youngsters could earn in several lifetimes. Safely deposited on the riverbank, the young man sprinted away from his companions. We felt so wretched watching that majestic beast float towards Egypt.

We didn't picnic during the summer months when the river floods and it's too hot to be out in the sun. Bathing, drinking, swimming—the Nile is within me to this day.

Departure

January 1988

"Let's go back home." I almost said it. My mind was in turmoil. I considered the impact on the rest of my life if I said it. I swallowed my words.

It was just past midnight. Daniel was driving us to the Khartoum International Airport on this winter night. Four-year-old Isabelle slept in the back seat. She won't remember this. She didn't understand we were leaving everything behind, including her dad.

Fresh air brushed the car windows on that night. A crescent moon, a symbol of this country where she was born, where we called home, shone through the car window. The streets were empty and quiet—just as we were.

My farewell gathering had ended an hour earlier. The dirty glasses and dishes were piled on the kitchen counter; the left-over food was put away. My sendoff party was an international event. Friends, from Cambodia to England, from Helsinki to Bombay, had come to say *maa salama*.

Our marriage was over, the property divided, the bank account split. I had held the moment of departure in my mind thousands of times. After twelve joyful yet challenging years, I was leaving Sudan for good. Leaving my marriage, my home, my friends, my job, my cats, my life. I remained silent.

We lived in a comfortable home in a pleasant neighborhood. We were a family; motherhood was my crowning achievement. The picture of my life was a masterpiece, but the paint was beginning to fade. Later I realized love for a man had turned into a passion for the country and the people of Sudan.

Daniel was the expatriate employee; I was the spouse who accompanied him. I worked on a local contract, paid by the hour. I could not afford to live on my own in Khartoum. A married woman lived with her husband. I could not live there separate from him.

Several months earlier, when taking off from the airport in Wau, a French journalist aboard the UNICEF plane began shouting, "They have rockets!"

A moment later, there was an explosion. Daniel checked his instruments; the plane's heading was stable. The missiles had missed the plane. They continued to Khartoum and landed safely. Daniel was still experiencing an adrenal rush when he got home.

"It was a near miss—a few feet more and the plane would have been taken out."

As we were having marriage problems at the time, my immediate thought was to the possible millions in insurance money I would have had. Did he sense my thoughts?

He stated, "You could have been a rich widow instead of a divorcee."

It was only a fleeting thought. But what if?

It was not unusual in the diplomatic corps in Sudan for the family to live in their home country while the husband worked abroad. Life was difficult; schooling was limited. Daniel and I didn't discuss our failed marriage with anyone other than our closest friends. Most people assumed Isabelle and I were leaving Khartoum so she could start school in California.

A year after our son died, we consulted a marriage counselor during our annual leave in California. He told Daniel and me that the death of a child would either make a marriage stronger or tear it apart. In my opinion, nothing was left. Apathy, the curse of any marriage, had taken root. I could only move forward in my life without Daniel.

The lust was long gone, the love was stale, and the loss of respect was the final straw. Daniel had changed. He blamed himself for the death of Xavier. He was convinced he was being punished for deeds committed in his younger years. He was morose and gloomy. His silliness, a trait so endearing, was buried with Xavier. I was his comfort. I was the glue keeping our lives together. He needed too much from me. I pitied him and no longer cared enough to help him climb out of his deep despair. I did not want to spend the rest of my life with him.

In the fall of 1987, I decided the marriage was over. I was ready to leave.

"Please stay until after the holidays," Daniel pleaded.

Four months to undo my life—to prepare for my future. I decided to finish my trip around the world, the journey I had begun twelve years earlier.

"Is it safe to travel with a young child?" he asked. "Leave Isabelle here with me and Saida. We'll come to California next summer. Then she can start school in America."

"No." I was adamant. "She'll go with me. The places we'll visit will be no more dangerous than Sudan."

I had a love-hate relationship with Sudan. Picnics on the Nile. Servants to help with the housework. I thrived on the challenges of different cultures and languages. Overcoming the difficulties of daily life made me stronger. The experience of living with both Sudanese and the international community had made me a citizen of the world.

During difficult times, I sat on our upstairs balcony, watching airplanes take off for Europe, wishing we were on that plane. Especially during extensive power outages, I pictured our family on a plane—a plane taking us away from Sudan for the last time. Now it

131

would be only Isabelle and me. My picture was of the whole family, not the broken one. Still, I was confident the future would be no worse than the present.

Sometimes I wonder how my life would have unfolded if I had not returned to Daniel after my visit to Egypt twelve years earlier. I have no regrets. For me, Sudan was a land of opportunities. My future volunteer work in Malawi, Ethiopia, and Cambodia was a direct result of the people I met and the experiences I had had in Sudan. I would not change anything except the accident in August 1985.

Sudan would be in my heart and would never leave me.

I drank from the Nile for the last time.

I'm glad I didn't say, "Let's go back home."

Epilogue

The sun crept over the Sierra Nevada Mountain range as Isabelle and I drove north down the mountains of the Grapevine where I–5 becomes SR 99. The April sunrise promised a clear day, bringing warmth and light to the fruit and vegetable crops grown in the San Joaquin Valley of California.

After a grueling twenty-seven hour flight from Bali to Los Angeles, we were on the way to Fresno, my childhood home where family and friends still resided. Our plane from Bali was delayed causing us to miss our connecting flight. Should we stay in the hotel offered by the airline? It was 11 p.m. in LA but midday in Bali. Therefore, I expected we would be awake all night. How would I entertain myself and five-year-old Isabelle until morning? I decided to rent a car and drive the four hours to Fresno, my old home. My new home?

After leaving Khartoum four months earlier, Isabelle and I had visited eight countries in southwest and southeast Asia. My daughter was the best travel companion. With her long blond hair and curious disposition, she opened many doors to fellow travelers and residents alike. A mother and young child, we were non-threatening and approachable. We traveled on buses, railroads, and airplanes. We visited tourist sites on ponies in the Himalayas, donkey carts in Burma, elephants in Thailand, rafts on the Mekong River, and tuk-tuks everywhere.

In India, she was called an angel. So many people asked to take her picture that she became shy and hid behind my skirt when she saw someone with a camera.

Riding ponies on the Annapurna trail in Nepal, she watched out for water buffalo, alerting our guide so the dangerous beasts wouldn't charge us. At Buddhist temples, she intuitively gathered her offerings, placed them on the altar, and knelt at the foot of the Buddha. How did she know to do this? In Thailand, she fed elephants and thus began her

life-long fascination with those fabulous creatures. At the Singapore Zoo, we had tea with an orangutan, and tropical birds roosted on our shoulders.

Now we would settle down and create a new life. Where would we live, where would I work, how would Isabelle adapt to life in California? How would I adjust without servants and nannies? This opportunity to start over came with the burden of making good choices.

I went back to school and earned a Master's in Business Administration. With my Clinical Laboratory Scientist license and my new M.B.A., I was hired as a Clinical Systems Administrator at Kaiser Permanente, Northern California. The work was challenging and rewarding. I was never bored, an excellent fit for me. I retired after twenty-five gratifying years.

I found a partner-in-everything, someone who touched my heart. Jim and I married and made our home in the rolling foothills of the Sierra Nevada Mountains. Outside my front door are miles of walking trails through the oaks and pines. For over twenty years, I have tended the vegetable garden, the fruit trees, and the poultry on our little farm.

Isabelle is working on a master's degree in Portland, Oregon. After thirty years in Africa, including ten years with UNICEF, Daniel retired and now resides in Thailand.

My childhood dreams had come true. I did trudge across the dunes of the African desert, watched the king of the beasts chase a gazelle, ascended the snowy mountain peaks of the Himalayas, strolled through the ancient bazaars in the Middle East, and climbed to the top of an Egyptian pyramid.

All my life experiences contributed to who I am—my joy, my contentment, and my serenity. I made the best of the opportunities that came my way.

Part Two

Thirty Years Later

2017

Home Coming

Once You Drink from the Nile, You Will Come Back Again
—A Sudanese Proverb

T'was the night before Christmas
When all through the house
All I could hear was the call from the mosque
—Isabelle, December 24th, 2017

Thomas Wolfe wrote *You Can't Go Home Again* in which the subject of the novel returns home to America and rediscovers it with love, sorrow, and hope.

I drank from the Nile for twelve years. It was my home. It was time to return. The river called me. Would I find love, sorrow, or hope?

Christmas of 2016 had been stressful. The week after the holidays, I placed Jim, my husband of twenty years, in a memory care facility. The stress landed me in the hospital for eight days with heart problems. While I was in the hospital, my ninety-two-year-old mother died from a stroke. I wanted to skip the holiday festivities in 2017. Sudan, a Muslim country, would be a perfect place to visit. No Christmas carols. No decorated trees. No festive lights and displays on front lawns.

Isabelle would be on break from her Master's degree program. Maybe she would like to go with me.

"Oh, yes, Mom! I'd love to see where I was born. And where we lived. I thought I'd never have an opportunity to do that!" she exclaimed.

She was four years old when we left. Would she remember anything?

CRSO

"Will everyone please remove their hand luggage from the overhead bin? Please check for any unrecognized item," came the announcement as my plane taxied for take-off from LAX to Istanbul. Two Turkish men wanted to get off the plane. Agitated and arguing in the aisle near the exit door, they would not return to their seats.

"Do you know what's going on?" I asked the handsome young man seated next to me.

"Nope, I'm Romanian. I don't know what those guys are yelling about. Do they think there's a bomb on the plane?"

Will he be the last person I see in my life? Will we hold hands during our final moments?

Our plane pulled out of the lineup for take-off. After a two-hour delay, still not knowing what had taken place, the cabin settled down—hand luggage safely stored, seat belts firmly buckled, tray tables in the upright position. Will I make my connection to Khartoum in Istanbul? Will I even arrive? What about Isabelle? Will she wait for me? She's flying to Istanbul from Portland, Oregon.

After thirteen uneventful hours, the plane touched down intact. Run—actually walk-as-fast-as-I-can—from my terminal to another terminal on the opposite side of the airport. Puffing. Anxious. How many flights go to Khartoum each day? Probably just one! And, most likely, not every day! Will Isabelle go without me? Has she arrived safely? I was supposed to arrive in Istanbul an hour before her.

Out of breath, through the duty-free shopping mall and multiple restaurants where the west terminal meets the east terminal, signs indicated a ten to thirty-minute walk to gates 201–222. I hoped the gate for Khartoum was the ten-minute walk. Gasping. Out of my way I signaled as I maneuver like a racecar driver through the throngs of other passengers, suitcases, baby strollers, and luggage carts.

There she was! Worry, uncertainty, torment on her face, Isabelle scanned the crowd of people rushing to their gates. Fortunately, our flight to Khartoum had been delayed; the last dozen passengers were boarding. I had made it!

"MOM!" she shouted. "I didn't know what to do! They said I would need to buy a new ticket if I didn't get on this flight. What happened to you?"

She didn't know who we were meeting in Khartoum. She thought she might have to spend the night at the airport. Anxiety filled her soul. She thought she might get lost in Africa. We gulped back tears as we embraced, celebrating our good fortune. One would think we hadn't seen each other in decades.

Our flight to Khartoum was uneventful, the landing rough. I had packed two suitcases with seventy-five pounds of gifts and twenty-five pounds of personal items. My blue bag full of gifts rolled out of the baggage tunnel onto the conveyer belt. Many more suitcases followed. Where was my brown suitcase, the one secured with a hot-pink luggage belt, the suitcase with all my personal items? All my carefully chosen articles I would need for our four-week visit. Round and round they went—no suitcase I recognized. Welcome to Sudan, the place where one must always expect the unexpected.

Filling out the Property Irregularity Report, I was told it would arrive *Bukra In'shalla*. Tomorrow, God willing. After the flight delay and the lost luggage report, I wondered if Suad would still be waiting for us. Would I recognize her? Would she know me? Suad, my friend and former work colleague, had invited us and was our official sponsor for our visas. And there she was, patiently waiting in the arrival terminal; we each recognized the other right away. She drove us to our apartment as the muezzin was calling the faithful to 4 a.m. prayer.

Earlier, on the plane, I read a book called *A Gentleman in Moscow,* about a Russian Count sentenced by a Bolshevik tribunal to house arrest in a hotel. Instead of his former elaborate suite, he must live in an attic room built for servants. The count postulates, "Can a life without luxury be the richest of all? ...a man must master his circumstances or be mastered by them."

I resolved to be the master of my circumstances. After all, I had lived in Sudan for twelve years; I can get through four weeks. Dressed in winter clothes on the plane, I surveyed the items I'd brought in my hand luggage—a skirt, a T-shirt, and extra underwear. What do I absolutely need for this 90° weather? Flip flops and sunscreen. We went shopping. I became the master of my circumstances.

Suad had rented an apartment for us close to where we used to live. It was walking distance to grocery stores, a pharmacy, restaurants, and other shops we would frequent during our stay. The apartment was small but functional, clean, and well furnished. A washing machine and cleaning supplies meant we were self-contained; no house servants needed.

Suad gave us her extra cell phone and an internet hot-spot as our American phones would not work in Sudan. As in all the world, everyone had a cell phone. And some had more than one.

"If you want to go anywhere, send a text to Tirhal. It's just like Uber. Here is their card. They'll know where you are from your text location and pick you up," she said.

My my, I was impressed. Khartoum had soared into the modern era. What else would astonish me?

The next day I wanted to visit the neighborhood where we had lived. Standing on the sidewalk outside our apartment, I sent a text message to Tirhal. Within minutes, a cream-colored sedan, a broken plastic "TAXI" sign in the middle of the front window, slowly pulled up to the curb where we were waiting. A young man with the cutest smile, looking expectant and giving Isabelle an obvious look-over, leaned over and opened the front passenger door for me. This must be our car from Tirhal.

"*Inta Tirhal?*" I asked in my halting Arabic.

"*Aiwa*" affirmed the handsome young man, getting out of the car to open the backseat door for Isabelle, giving her his most charming smile.

That was too easy. Ever the skeptic, I am, nevertheless, delighted when things work well. In my limited Arabic, I told him where we wanted to go and that I wanted a driver who would stay with us all day while we visited our former neighborhood. He said I spoke Arabic well; I disagreed; however, I was finding the words I thought I had forgotten.

First, we went to the German Club on Street One. Memories flooded back as we walked around the garden. How many hundreds of dinners had we eaten there with friends, friends who are still dear to my heart? The crystal clear water in the swimming pool looked inviting. We asked if we could have a membership for the duration of our stay.

Across the street from the club should be the Air Taxi Rest House. I didn't recognize anything. I was sure of the placement and tried to peek through the security gate. It didn't look like where we had lived.

Of course, the trees and bushes were much taller, obscuring the view, but the building did not appear to be the one where we had lived. This building was five stories high. More memories flooded my mind—the little third-floor room with my potted pepper plant where bullets zinged past my head on the Fourth of July.

Next, we visited the Khartoum Clinic where Isabelle was born. The building was undergoing major renovations—we were not able to go inside. Again, memories of pain and joy overcame me. We took some photos and obtained the phone number of Dr. Sayda Dirdry, the doctor who delivered Isabelle thirty-four years ago. We tried, but unfortunately, we were unable to make contact with her.

I didn't recognize our home on Thirty-Seventh Street. The first corner from the Cemetery Road. This had to be it. But the surrounding wall, entrance, and building were different. The building, then two stories high, now rose four stories. It seemed like the city was growing up in many ways.

The building was now a private primary school. The teachers in the playground invited us in. This had to be the right place. Then I saw the doors! The same entryway—frosted glass with iron grating on the outside. Daniel would open them up and secure his motorcycle inside those doors every night.

The teachers invited us inside to see the school. The stairway so familiar; I had climbed those stairs thousands of times. With tears in my eyes, we ascended the steps to the rooms where Isabelle grew up. Some of the walls had been moved; our bedrooms are now classrooms. The balcony, where I had watched airplanes taking off from the runway, was closed in as another classroom. I showed Isabelle where she crawled and where she took her first steps, her first bedroom, the kitchen where I had bathed her in the sink. This was the place where we became a family. Where love surrounded us. Where hope and expectations bloomed. Where sadness and grief overtook us.

Isabelle at the doors

ᏚᎯᎲᎲᎣ

The Tirhal driver's name was Mohailen and, by the end of the day, after many miles and numerous selfies, he and Isabelle became Facebook friends. He spoke no English, but Mohailen was an excellent driver—helpful and considerate. His car was in good repair. Plus, his air conditioner worked. I didn't know how much to pay him, and he didn't know how much I should pay. It should have been a clue to the information I would learn much later. I gave him a wad of bills, and he gave most of it back to me, keeping about four dollars' worth of Sudanese money. He had spent most of the day with us. I didn't think four dollars was enough. What do people earn these days? What is the cost of living? Nevertheless, I felt safe with him and decided we would text him directly next time we needed a ride.

ᏚᎯᎲᎲᎣ

After five days, my brown suitcase with the hot-pink luggage belt arrived; my summer clothing—sandals, pants, short sleeve blouses, my books, my green tea, and my toiletries. I did not need to test the theory, "Can a life without luxury be the richest of all?"

Karmakol

A few days later, we were on our way north to Karmakol, a small village not even identified on Google Maps.

The trigger for our visit to Sudan was the first-ever Karmakol International Cultural Festival. Suad had sent me an internet link to the festival, and the video captured my heart. The Swiss Initiative, the sponsor of this festival, promised "music, theater, film, arts, and literature under the sky of Karmakol." Located over 200 miles north of Khartoum, this festival, ending twenty years of cultural isolation, was to be a celebration of workshops and performances. Questions popped into my mind. How can you have a festival, expecting over 500 artists and guests, in the middle of nowhere, in a village of two thousand people, a five-hour drive from any major town, desert all around? What about food, fuel, electricity, housing?

Trusting the reputation for Swiss efficiency, I bought tickets to this festival and planned our return to the Nile.

Suad did not want Isabelle and me, being women and foreigners, to travel out of town alone with a male Sudanese driver. She helped me hire a driver who knew the area and had a four-wheel-drive vehicle. Suad also arranged for three young Sudanese to accompany us to Karmakol. Soon after leaving Khartoum, we stopped at a small market where colorful donkey carts filled the parking area. Our companions bought sodas and potato chips for the drive; Isabelle and I bought a bag of *tahamiya* (aka falafel) from a vendor who fried them on his charcoal brazier along the street. He smiled at us and not only allowed us to take his photo, but he also posed in various stages of the food preparation so we could document the entire process. Afterward, he whipped out his cell phone to take a selfie with us.

The further from town we got, the lighter the traffic. Soon we were passing donkey carts, camel drivers, sheepherders, and flocks of goats that ran wild. Newly paved, the road was smooth, wide enough for two cars, but with no shoulder. The desert encroached from both sides. We passed a couple of rickety buses with people hanging out the door.

The dry, undulating landscape soon gave way to a flat, parched stretch of sand—sand in every direction. The sun, in the crisp, cloudless sky, provided welcomed warmth on this December morning.

We were in the Nubian Desert, the eastern region of the Sahara. The few homes, made from mud bricks, had flat roofs and were spaced far apart. They all looked the same. Most homes had a boma, a kind of corral constructed of tree branches, near the house to confine the family's livestock—donkeys or camels, goats, and sheep. The camels, often mean and ornery, were always kept in separate pens. Acacia trees dotted the landscape.

Water wells were spaced many miles apart. The water was pumped into black and white checked storage tanks on stilts fifty feet in the air, visible for miles. What supplied power to the pumps? I hope it was solar, modern technology applied to an age-old practice. Every so often, we would see a young lad on a donkey pulling a cart fixed with a fifty-gallon drum going to or from the tank delivering water to the homes in the area. Well-worn tire tracks to the tanks meant the well and pumps were operational.

About an hour out of Khartoum, we came to a military checkpoint. Huge oil drums on the road funneled us into one lane. A pole weighted with a cement slab blocked the way. After a quick glance inside our vehicle, the guards directed us to pull off the road. Bakri, our driver, handed over a copy of our passports and travel documents which were carefully inspected by a smartly uniformed guard. Another guard, armed with a rifle, opened the back of the land cruiser and gruffly asked our companion, Ahmed, some questions. Not satisfied with the answers, the guard commanded Ahmed to step out of the car. We all got out as it looked like we might get a thorough inspection.

Arabic can be a soft, sweetly-spoken language. However, in this case, the words were sharp, loud, and forceful. I had no idea what was going on. The look on the face of the officer was not friendly. Ahmed handed his open soda can to the officer who sniffed the can then dumped some of the liquid into his hand. He brought his hand to his nose, then quickly splashed the liquid onto the ground. Next, he opened our ice chest to inspect the contents. We were ordered to get back in the car. As we drove off, our Sudanese companions started laughing. We asked what was so funny; it sure didn't feel like an amusing situation to me. It turned out the officer thought there was beer in the soda can. Can't be too careful in a country where alcoholic beverages are prohibited.

On we drove, hour after hour, sand and more sand. I recalled the time I was stranded on a broken-down train in this very area. The further north we went, the colder it got. The acacia trees gave way to leafless bushes hugging the ground until even they could not survive the arid desert. The color of the sand changed from coral to buttery-yellow.

Houses were few and far between. The desiccated white bones of whole animal carcasses dotted the roadside. How can people survive out here? Obviously, some animals can't. Far off the road, black rocks appeared on the hills in the distance. I wish I had studied geology. I wanted to know where the rocks came from, and why does the sand change color? The changes in the landscape were subtle yet definite.

After several hours of driving, Bakri said, "We will visit an aunt's house, have lunch, and then, soon after lunch, we will arrive in Karmakol."

What a pleasant surprise! I was pleased. We would eat a typical Sudanese meal at one of these houses off the road. Twenty minutes later, he drove off the main road onto the hard-packed sand. We pulled up to a lone ant hill, six feet tall. We all got out and took some photos. I tried to show enthusiasm. What a disappointment when I realized he meant "ant," not "aunt."

Within a half-hour, we arrived at the festival. We checked in and realized, other than the small European staff, we were the only non-Sudanese people there. And yet, after decades of sanctions and isolation from the Western world, we were treated as honored guests. From the time of my arrival in Sudan over forty years ago, I have noted the Sudanese are the most gracious people in the world.

We enjoyed the river, the breeze, the date palm groves, and the sand. We took a boat to an island in the middle of the river. We visited the ruins of the old village where artwork was displayed on the crumbling walls. We visited the reconstructed ancient Nubian home, recently on display in Italy. We shopped at the women's' handicraft exhibition.

My thoughts turned to my family and friends during this frantic, feverish, and frenzied holiday season at home. I was grateful to miss it this year.

The first night, the blaring twang of a guitar announced the start of the evening's entertainment. Hundreds of red plastic chairs facing the stage were hastily occupied—women seated on the left, men on the right. When all the seats were taken, hundreds of men stood behind the seats. Where did all these people come from? The music ranged from quiet traditional Sudanese music to contemporary rock 'n' roll. The audience was enthusiastic and well-mannered, keeping the front of the stage and the aisles clear as directed by the security staff.

The next night, the crowd was equally courteous until the featured band started to play. The group, named Imarhan from Algeria, brought down the house and brought up the crowd. Arms in the air, fingers snapping, hands clapping, smiles, whooping and hollering. There was a mad rush to the front of the stage and the aisles filled with dancing, swaying men and women. The audience was ecstatic. The security staff gave up. The musicians, six young men in long white robes, two guitars, one bass, one djembe, and one water gourd, pumped out rhythms that went straight to the heart—smiles, happiness, excitement. Even the now-empty chairs seemed to move with the beat. This was worth the cost, the discomforts, and the apprehension of this excursion. Let the good times roll. I wanted to be nowhere else. Let the music play all night long.

Khartoum

Back in Khartoum, Mohailen picked us up most mornings to take us on outings. We stood on the bank where the Blue and White Nile rivers meet, becoming The Nile flowing gently to Egypt. We drove over the bridge to Tuti Island where we hired a boat to take us around the island. The crops growing in the recently flooded ground were now irrigated with diesel engines pumping water from the river. Gone were the leather buckets swinging from poles. When our boat ran out of gas, we floated down the river. Fortunate for cell phones and friends with extra gas, we were soon on our way around the island. Gone were the feluccas piloted by expert sailors.

We were warned not to swim in the Blue Nile as Bilharzia was now found there. We walked along the old Blue Nile Bridge where Daniel had proposed marriage to me while I rode on the back of his motorcycle. The army guards stationed on the bridge smiled in greeting and posed with us for selfies, their machine guns across their chests.

Mohailen took us for meals at neighborhood eateries that most likely had never served a white customer. We were well received, and warmly welcomed. After sharing many miles and cups of tea, Mohailen became not only our driver, but also our tour guide, negotiator, and friend.

We made many new friends, mostly young women working with Suad in medical research. We were invited to dinner parties and tea. The few European people working in Sudan, young volunteers working for NGOs (non-governmental organizations), had parents visit over the holidays. When Isabelle was asked if her mom was visiting her, she replied, "No, I was born here. We're both visiting Sudan. I want to see where I grew up."

"Oh, then you are Sudanese," was the typical reply. "Maybe you will come back after you finish school to work here. We need your help."

This pleased Isabelle immensely. Would I want Isabelle to work in Sudan? Immediately, my response would be an emphatic Yes! Sudan was good to both her father and me. He had the best jobs of his career. I had gained confidence, self-assurance, and sophistication from living there. Could Isabelle find the same?

೦೩ಐ

"I'm downstairs," said the message on my phone from Samia. Without a doorbell, *WhatsApp* worked well for communication—when the internet worked.

As we walked down the hallway between our two buildings, a white car pulled up, and the passenger door was opened.

"Samia?" I asked.

"Yes," stated the driver.

Mmm… I thought Samia was a woman. Arrangements had been made for someone to pick us up and take us to the Michigan State University Laboratory, still a functioning research lab in the Stack Building downtown where I used to work.

I asked the driver as we eased into traffic, "Did I work with you?"

"Maybe I took you to the airport," he stated.

"No, I recently arrived. You didn't take me to the airport."

"I'm a driver during the day, I work at the airport in the evenings," he stated.

Oh well, someone, (Samia or Suad?) must have sent a driver to get us.

"You know where the Stack Lab is?" I asked.

"Oh, sure," he said in perfect English.

Inching through the morning rush hour traffic that lasts until late afternoon, our driver skillfully maneuvered his car downtown, averting what seemed like inevitable fender-benders. His cell phone rang insistently; he ignored it. We also ignored the street vendors shoving mangoes, tea sets, and car parts through our open window. About thirty minutes and four miles later, crossing the train tracks signaling the start of downtown, something didn't seem right.

"The Stack Lab is that way," I said, pointing to the left.

"Yes, it is," he stated but continued driving straight ahead.

A few minutes later, when I knew we were going the wrong way, I asked again, "Do you know where the Stack Lab is?"

Again, "Yes."

"But you're going the wrong way. I want to go to the Stack Lab."

"No, I am taking you to UNDP."

"No, I am going to the Stack Lab."

"Aren't you Dan?" he asked me?

"No, my name is Sheila. Didn't Samia send you?"

Embarrassed, he turned around and took us to the Stack Lab. He refused any compensation for the error. I wonder how long Dan waited for his driver. Too bad Mohailen hadn't driven us, he would have known where to take us.

Weeks later, we found out Mohailen was not a driver and did not work for Tirhal. He owned a repair shop for car air conditioners near our apartment. Business was slow in the winter. He just happened to drive by our apartment while we waited for Tirhal. He must have done a double-take when he saw a young white woman standing on the sidewalk looking for a ride. He had stopped to see if he could help us. Later he saw a possible ticket to America. Never mind his wife and two little boys. In friendship, he saw us off at the airport before our midnight departure—with hugs but no kisses.

CRLSO

I want the world to know how cordial, gracious, and generous the Sudanese people are. Walking from the source of the White Nile in

Rwanda to the delta in Egypt, Levison Wood writes in his book *Walking the Nile,* "But it is not for nothing that the Sudanese are hailed, the world over, as the most hospitable of hosts." I could not agree more.

Tea Lady

Walking around town, we often sat down to have a cup of tea with the tea ladies who set up shop under the shade of trees. No longer did these women sport facial scars and tattoos like the previous generation. According to tribal customs, women would permanently ink their lower lips or have scars running from cheekbone to chin. I was glad to see these customs have stopped, although it seems like these practices have moved to the Western world.

Waiting for our tea, we sat on child-like plastic stools. The tea ladies' tables each contained a charcoal burner with hot water at the ready, tea, sugar, glasses, and a soapy washing bucket. I received looks of astonishment when I requested *shaay biduun sukkar* (tea without sugar). In a flash, our steamy tea was brewed and poured into the clean glasses. We leisurely sipped our tea, engaging the tea lady with bits of conversation, in Arabic, of course. Usually, when ready to depart, payment was refused. We were honored guests, not paying guests. Flashing smiles, the women were always gracious to submit to a photo with us, grooming their hair and adjusting their *toubs* before we snapped the picture.

Generosity is a cultural trait at all economic levels. Although it felt awkward, I gratefully accepted these gifts with the affection in which they were given.

CRICO

Separation and Sanctions—I heard these two words often in conversation.

Since 1997, the citizens had suffered under the sanctions imposed by the USA, the European Union, and the United Nations. The government was known for its continued support for international terrorism, relentless efforts to destabilize neighboring governments, and human rights violations. Designed to cripple the government of Sudan, the sanctions also blocked the assets of Sudanese citizens. Travel bans were imposed. My Sudanese friends no longer had access to their bank accounts in England or the USA. Professionals could no longer attend international conferences. Visits to or from family members outside of Sudan stopped.

In 2011, following decades of civil war with the north, southern Sudan voted to separate from the north. South Sudan became the youngest country on the planet. No longer would Sudan be the largest country in Africa; that title now belongs to Algeria. No longer would oil reserve money pour into the northern coffers. How would the national debt be divided? How would citizenship be established— location or tribal affiliation? Chaos ensued in both the north and the south as power shifted.

These two significant events changed the lives of the people I know. Feeling powerless and frustrated, making do with what little they had, finding new ways to make ends meet, the people were discouraged. Known for their generosity, their kindness, and their optimism, they felt like they had hit rock bottom.

CR&SO

I had returned home. I found love for the people, sorrow for their circumstances, and hope for their future. I left a piece of my heart there.

At a dinner party near the end of our stay, I quoted the saying about returning to the Nile. A university professor, close to retirement age, said, "I drank from the Nile all my life and I never left. And if I did, I would NOT return."

We all laughed. So much for the proverb, but for me—Once you drink from the Nile, you will come back again—it held true.

Acknowledgments

To Pam Smedley, I thank you for your encouragement to make a few stories into a book. To my fellow writers at Pam's Writing Gym, I thank you for your support, your observations, and your backing that kept me going when I wanted to give up. A special note of gratitude to Peg Smith, Tim Broader, and Penny Ross, who reviewed my manuscript before I called it a book; your input is valued.

A singular toast of gratitude goes to Jan Camp of Arc Light Books, who provided me with valuable assistance.

A big thanks to all the people, friends, and family, who, over the years, read sections and provided meaningful feedback to me.

Special thanks go to the people of Sudan. My time there greatly enriched my life. A special thanks to Suad Sulaiman who will always be a special friend.

Glossary

Aiwa Yes

Al-Hamdu lillah Thanks to God

Angrareeb a rope bed

Bent Girl

Bukra, **In'shalla** Tomorrow, God willing

Harami Thief

Inta quayse Are you well?

Jebena a container used to brew coffee in the Eritrean and Ethiopian traditional coffee ceremony

Jelabiya Traditional long, white male robe

Kwawaaja Male foreigner, usually of European descent

Leben Milk

Maa Salama Good-bye

Mulukhiyah a vegetable dish made from the leaves of a jute plant

Salaam alaykum Peace be unto you – a greeting

Toub a traditional, long piece of thin cloth women wrap around the body and over the head.

Wa'alaykum as-salaam And unto you peace – response to a greeting

Zehir Conical clay pot for drinking water

Sheila Van der Smissen Larsen lives with her husband and two cats in the foothills east of Fresno, California. Reading, farming, hiking, and camping keeps her busy in retirement. She still enjoys international travel and has visited ten countries on four continents in the past two years.

If you crossed paths with her somewhere in the world, she would like to hear from you.

Contact her at
drinkingfromthenile@gmail.com

Made in the USA
Middletown, DE
17 January 2023

21644911R00109